yabu pushelberg

55 BOOTH AVENUE TORONTO CANADA M4M 2M3 416/778-9779 FAX 778-9747

# Steps

# Steps &

# Steps & Stairways

Cleo Baldon
Ib Melchior

*with* Julius Shulman
*Photographic Consultant*

NEW YORK

First published in the United States of America in
1989 by Rizzoli International Publications, Inc.
300 Park Avenue South, New York, NY 10010

Library of Congress Cataloging-in-Publication Data

Baldon, Cleo.
 Steps and Stairways / by Cleo Baldon and Ib
Melchior : photographic consultant, Julius Shulman.
 p. cm.
 ISBN 0-8478-1075-5
 1. Stairs. 2. Staircases. I. Melchior, Ib. II. Shulman,
Julius. III. Title.
NA3060.b34 1989

721'.832—dc19          89-30286 CIP

STEPS & STAIRWAYS
was produced for
Rizzoli International Publications, Inc.
by Perpetua Press, Los Angeles

Edited by LETITIA BURNS O'CONNOR
Designed by DANA LEVY

Typeset in Palatino by Wilsted & Taylor,
Oakland
Printed and bound in Hong Kong

PAGE 1
**Primitive rock stairway leading toward the Teng-
boche Mountain in Nepal.**

PAGE 2–3
**Steps in the magnificent fourth-century B.C. theater
at Epidaurus in Greece.**

PAGE 4–5
**Utility and art come together in this red granite
staircase in the lobby of the Deutsche Bank in
Frankfurt, West Germany, designed by architects
Charles Pfister and Robinson Mills & Williams.**

**The forecourt area of the town hall and civic center ▷
in Sunderland, England, is built on different
levels and contains sophisticated transitions of
steps and slopes using brick-faced stair treads and
geometric paving, which creates a pleasing pattern
and incorporates handicap ramping. Architects,
John S. Bonnington Partnership.**

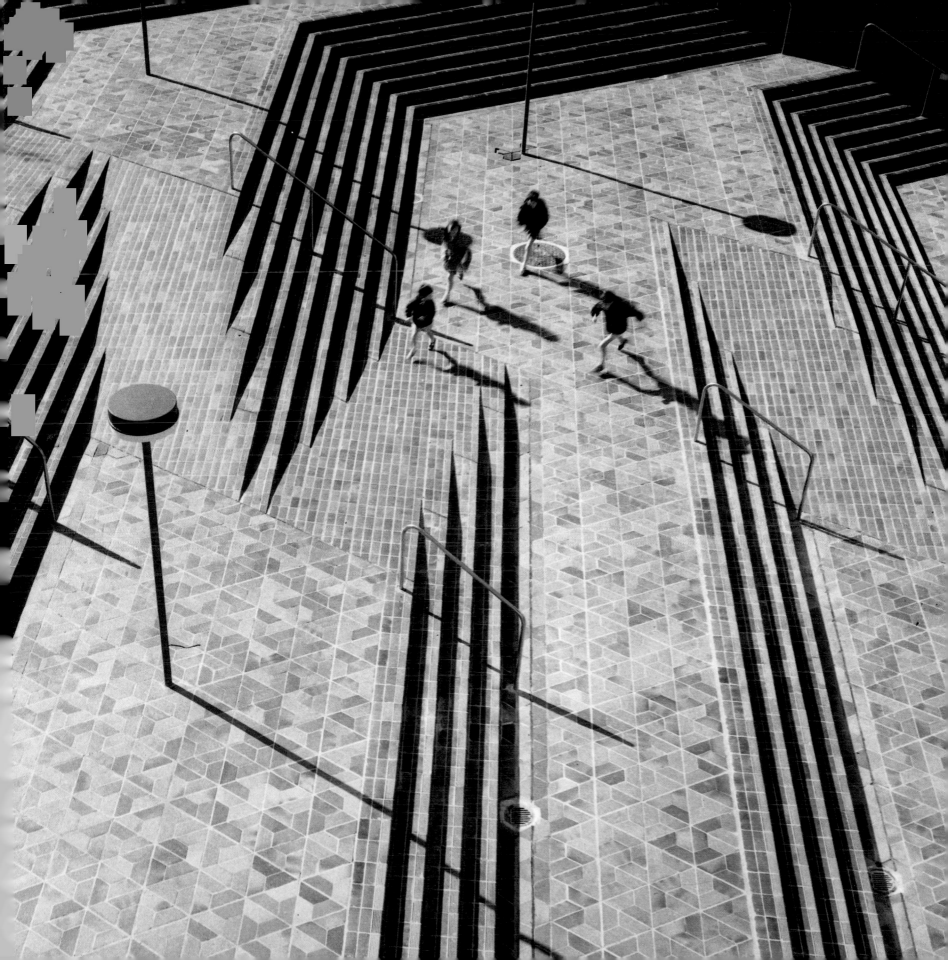

# Contents

*To our many friends,*
*all of whom*
*had a favorite stairway*
*to contribute.*

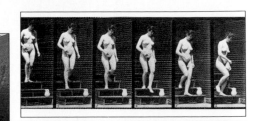

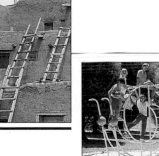

Stairs leading to the pulpit
entrance in the interdenomi-
national chapel at Miramar
Naval Air Station in California, designed by Richard
Neutra in 1957.

<small>Opposite</small>
In Wells Cathedral, Somer-
set, England, two great
flights of irregular stairs
converge. This justly famous
photograph, taken in 1903
by British photographer
Frederic Henry Evans,
renowned for his studies of
cathedrals in England and
France, is called *A Sea of
Steps*.

# 1 Introduction: The Stairway Defined

**W**hen early man first clambered up a tree to escape a charging beast he discovered the importance of being able to get up. Since that time his descendants have sought ways to improve this necessary maneuver both in method and design. The evolution from the first branched tree trunk to the gleaming chrome circular escalator that sweeps passengers from floor to floor is long and fascinating.

In the dark forests of prehistory, the only way for man to get up was to climb a tree, alternating hand over foot, hand over foot, like the bears and monkeys. The tree with its footholds of branches was a tower for watching, a place of safety above the danger of marauding animals. When a tree fell it could be dragged to a steep rock wall and propped at an angle to give access to an otherwise out-of-reach cave.

Was it then a stairway? Or was it a ladder after it was shorn of foliage and the branches trimmed short to accommodate the width of the foot that climbed upon them? How many generations passed before the next invention, steps, came about? An ancient stair type from Africa of unremembered time is made from a log hacked off at an angle at one end and placed with that angled slice on the ground. At regular intervals it was hewn in V-shaped gouges like a ratchet. Placed at a slant, one leg of each notch was parallel to the floor, becoming the tread. The other leg of the notch, at right angle to the first, became the riser. What a graceful and practical ladder it was.

At Lejre, on the island of Sjaelland in Denmark, there is a meticulous reconstruction of a village from the Iron Age (500 B.C.–A.D. 800), which stood there some two thousand years ago. A slanted log, gouged in tread and riser in the same way as the ancient African ladder, is used to reach the loft in a thatched-roof longhouse.

In such a village of long ago, might the evolution of steps not have happened in the following way? In the primitive hut that served as a carpenter's shop in the winter, perhaps two such log ladders had been made for the neighbors—one in exchange for grain, the other for the haunch of a deer. They stood next to each other, at the same slant and with gouges much the same, for their maker was a craftsman. When his woman brought him food, finding the work stone cluttered, she might have put a flattened piece of log across the gouges from ladder to ladder. At the sight of it he added other flat pieces, climbing upon them to reach something stored above, and it was a staircase. Evidence and logic suggest that similar incidents must have occurred in other places at other times: these inventions could not have been single events, but a universal discovery to be made when the time was ripe. Once the stairway had evolved, all that was left for future generations to invent was the handrail, the banister. After that all other additions were embellishments.

It is not without reason that the stairway is called a *flight*, for by it, foot over foot, earthbound man may rise to the height of birds. The stairway consists of treads and risers and something to hold them. There is much variety in that holding of steps and infinite elaboration on their surroundings, colors, and materials. But the geometry of the steps themselves, which is based on the proportion of the human body and its walking stride, varies

**This sketch for a staircase by Leonardo da Vinci (1452–1519) shows his experimentation with designs for elaborate and intricate stairways, although they were never realized.**

only slightly. The similarity of certain painted images, shapes of boats, weaving motifs, or elephant carvings where no elephant ever lived, has led to speculation about encounters between civilizations in ancient times. No such speculation occurs because of the sameness of steps the world over. They are simply the upward extension of people walking, their proportions and configuration controlled by human size.

The first-century B.C. Roman architect Vitruvius defined what makes some stairs more comfortable than others in *De Architectura*, recording his views on the best combination of treads and risers to a temple. "The rise of such steps should, I think, be limited to not more than ten inches (25.5 cm) nor less than nine inches (23 cm); for then the ascent will not be difficult. The treads of the steps ought to be made not less than a foot and a half (46 cm), and not more than two feet deep (61 cm)."

The seventeenth-century English diplomat and writer Sir Henry Wotton (1568–1639) recorded his opinon that: "To make a compleate Staire-case is a curious peece of Architecture." And he cautioned that "The breadth of every single Step or Staire bee never lesse than one foote (30.5 cm), nor more than eighteen inches (46 cm)," and "that they exeede by no meanes halfe a foot (15 cm) in their height or thickness; for our Legges doe labor more in Elevation, than in Distension."

Jacques-François Blondel (1705–74), author of the influential theoretical work *Cours d'architecture*, concluded that the stride or pace of walking was 24 in. (61 cm) and that when negotiating a stairway this pace should be decreased in proportion to the height of the riser. His theory was that two times the height of the riser plus the depth of the tread should equal the 24 in. of the pace. Thus he recommended that a 5 in. (12.5 cm) riser should have a 14 in. (35.5 cm) tread; a 6 in. (15 cm) riser, a 12 in. (30.5 cm) tread; and a 7

Notched log ladder in a longhouse at the reconstructed Iron-Age village at Lejre, Denmark.

Model of a Stone-Age flint mine in North Jutland, Denmark.

◁  Notched log ladder in an old Japanese storehouse on Okinoerabu Island in the East China Sea.

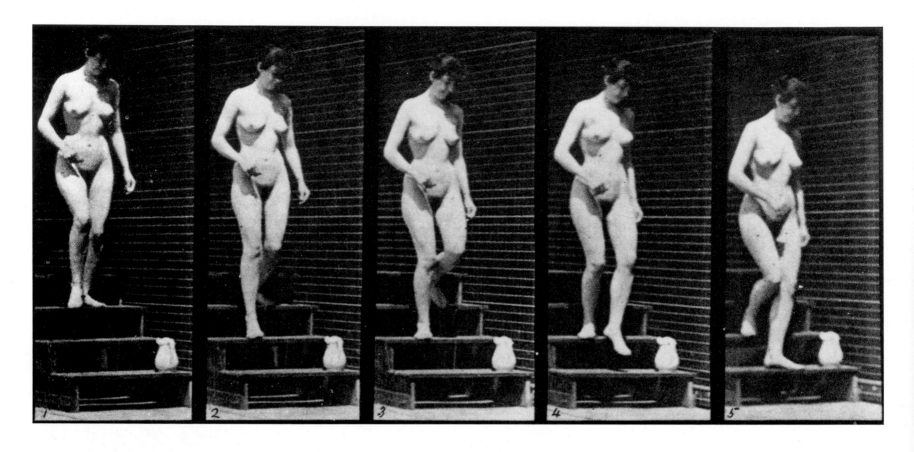

This 1885 study of a nude woman descending a flight of stairs is from the monumental work *Muybridge's Complete Human and Animal Locomotion*, an encyclopedic, photographic study of anatomy in motion by Eadweard Muybridge (1830–1904). Using electrically controlled cameras, Muybridge was able to freeze motion in series and study the body positions of men and women ascending and descending a variety of steps and stairs, stools and ladders. The more than 1,800 images of stairway ascents show that the knee remains bent for an entire flight of stairs.

OPPOSITE

A potent influence on diverse antitraditional arts of the mid-twentieth century, French-born Marcel Duchamp (1887–1968) portrayed human motion in several paintings: the first, *Sad Young Man in a Train*; the most famous, *Nude Descending a Staircase No. 1*, 1911, shown here. He returned to this theme in 1912, refining and developing further the swirling, interlocking lines of his subject in *Nude Descending a Staircase, No. 2*.

in. (18 cm) riser, a 10 in. (25.5 cm) tread. The Blondel theory is invalid at both extremes, for at one end a riser of less than 4 in. (10 cm) tends to trip the climber, and at the other, anything shallower than an 11 in. (28 cm) tread would not accommodate many of the feet for which it was intended.

Recently a California landscape architecture firm, Galper/Baldon Associates, measured the pace of every staff member and that of several passers-by, marking their strides in chalk on the sidewalk to establish a standard interval for the placement of stepping stones. The research revealed that a 26 in. (66 cm) pace is standard, which corresponds to today's widely accepted formula of two times the riser plus the tread equalling 26 in. This formula allows for a 4 in. (10 cm) riser with an 18 in. (46 cm) tread; the

minimum 11 in. (28 cm) tread would have a riser of 7.5 in. (19 cm). These are acceptable limits of comfortable ascent and descent of stairs. Exterior steps and stairs should be on the low riser/deep tread end of the scale, for the outdoor stride is freer of constraint.

In an experiment published in *Scientific American* in 1974, replicas of existing stairways of different proportions were made and people were photographed ascending and descending them. The first stairway replicated in the study, one of those at Lincoln Center in New York City, had four risers leading from the front door of the Metropolitan Opera to the plaza. The risers were 3.5 in. (8.5 cm) high and the treads were 25 in. (63.5 cm) deep, producing a 32 in. (80.5 cm) stride equivalent, too long for comfort. Because of the awkward gait imposed on the

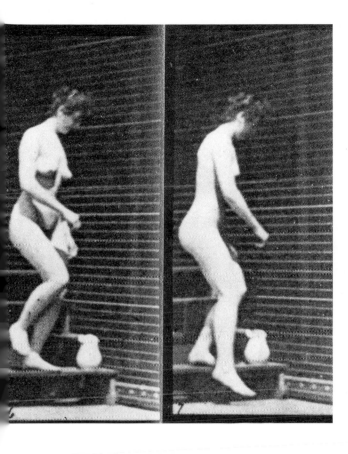

climber, missteps and accidents occurred on these stairs. Descending them was particularly hazardous since such low risers may not be seen. The hazardous condition at Lincoln Center has since been corrected: the poorly designed steps were replaced with a ramp. The experiment concluded that the optimum measurements should be risers from 4 to 7 in. (10 to 18 cm) high with treads from 11 in. (30 cm) to 14 in. (35.5 cm) deep to assure the lowest rate of energy expenditure and the least number of missteps.

Disproportionate steps within a flight of stairs can trip the person ascending or cause the descending one to fall down the stairs. There is an often repeated story that in the spiral staircase leading to a sleeping room in the Tower of London one riser is higher than the others and is supposed to trip the would-be assassin,

Body postures are markedly different when ascending or descending a shallow stairway or a steep one, as demonstrated by these two women, one strolling down a stair-street in Mykonos, Greece, the other struggling up a pyramid at Chichén Itzá, Mexico.

who, presumably with rich oaths and other commotion, would wake up his intended victim. The Education Officer at the Royal Armory of the Tower of London, however, pointedly suggests that trusted servants and locked doors might offer better protection. He disclaims knowledge of any such disproportionate riser there and theorizes that such flaws are probably due to faulty workmanship rather than devious intention.

At the Forest Cemetery in Stockholm, four long flights of stairs with broad landings between, designed by Sigurd Lewerentz in 1932, climb an open grassy slope to a meditation garden. After each landing the height of the riser on the new flight of stairs is slightly decreased and the depth of the tread increased, resulting in a change of pace and perhaps of mood as well.

To the father of psychoanalysis, Sigmund Freud, steps and stairs mean something quite different: they are symbolic representations of the sex act.

We directed our investigations to the occurrence in dreams of flights of stairs, ladders and steps, and we soon ascertained that stairs, or anything analogous to them, represent a definite symbol of coitus. The basis for this comparision is not difficult to find; with rhythmical intervals and increasing breathlessness one reaches a height, and may then come down again in a few rapid jumps. Thus the rhythm of coitus is reproduced in climbing stairs. Let us not forget to consider the colloquial usage. This tells us that "mounting" is, without further addition, used as a substitutive designation for the sexual act.

Children must negotiate a stairway with extreme care since its proportions are not well suited to short legs.

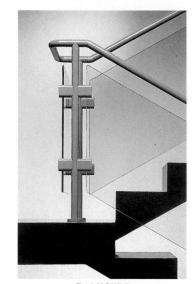
ALTERNATE
STEPS

BANISTER

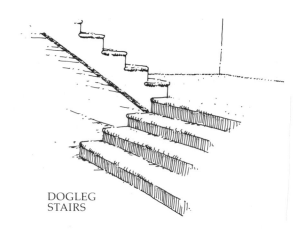
DOGLEG
STAIRS

BALUSTRADE

CURTAIL
STEP

The subject of steps and stairs has a rich nomenclature, but a survey of dictionaries and encylopedias also reveals contradictory definitions within this terminology, which this glossary addresses.

| | |
|---|---|
| ALTERNATE STEPS | Stairs in which the individual treads do not run the entire width of the stairway, but alternate to provide separate steps for the right and left foot of the climber |
| BALUSTER | One of a set of small pillars supporting a handrail |
| BALUSTRADE | A handrail supported by a row of balusters |
| BANISTER | A handrail or balustrade along a staircase or stairwell |
| BRIDGEBOARD | *See* String or Stringers |
| CARRIAGE | The entire supporting framing, including stringers |
| CURTAIL STEP | The curved bottom step of a stairway, which extends beyond the width of the stairs |
| DOGLEG STAIRS | Two straight flights running in parallel but opposite direction with a landing between |
| DOUBLE STAIRCASE | Two associated stairway flights reaching the same level at top and bottom |
| FLIGHT | A series of steps, uninterrupted by landings |
| FLYERS | Rectangular treads uniform in width and parallel |
| GEOMETRICAL STAIRCASE | Steps built into wall at one end, each step supported by the step below |
| HANDRAIL | A railing of a convenient height to be grasped for support when ascending or descending a stairway; a barrier at the edge of a stairway or balcony, etc. |
| HOLD | Any protrusion or indentation designed to be grasped when ascending or descending a stairway |
| LANDING | A platform between flights of steps that allows the climber to rest, or makes it possible for a stairway to change direction; its size should be at least the width of a tread plus a stride |
| NEWEL | The central supporting column of a spiral stairway; a post that terminates the handrail at the foot or at the head of a staircase or at a landing |

DOUBLE
STAIRCASE

QUADRUPLE
STAIRCASE

NEWEL

| | |
|---|---|
| NOSING | The frontal projection of the tread beyond the riser |
| PITCH | The degree of incline. A pitch over 45 degrees is not easy to climb, and one under 27 degrees is tedious and slow. |
| QUADRUPLE STAIRCASE | Four stairways around a rectilinear core |
| RIGHT-LEFT STEPS | *See* Alternate Steps |
| RISER | The vertical member of a step |
| RUN | Distance between the stair-head and the stairfoot of a stairway |
| SINGLE-STEP STAIRS | *See* Alternate Steps |
| SPIRAL STAIRCASE | A set of wedge-shaped steps arranged in a circular plan to wind around a newel or a central well |
| STAIRCASE | The entire structure housing a flight or flights of steps including the supporting framework, landings, balusters, handrail, etc. |
| STAIRFOOT | The level space in front of the lowest step of a stairway |

| | |
|---|---|
| STAIRHEAD | The level space at the top of a stairway |
| STAIRS | A series of steps mounted on a slant one above the other, sometimes interrupted by platforms known as landings |
| STAIRWAY | Stairs supported by an incline, made of either natural or artificial materials, or by a man-made structure. Stairway is the catch-all term for any system of steps. |
| STRING or STRINGER | One of the inclined sides of a stair supporting the treads and risers, usually used in pairs. Also called a bridge-board. A *closed stringer* has a side board covering the ends of the treads and risers; an *open stringer* shows the end of the tread· a *cut stringer* is notched on its upper edge to receive the tread. |
| TREAD | The horizontal surface of a step |
| WINDER | A uniformly curved stairs or a triangular or wedge-shaped tread used to turn corners |
| WREATH | A curved handrail or stringer or the curved portion thereof |

NOSING

CLOSED
STRINGER

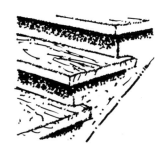

OPEN
STRINGER

Winick Photo

View in Pueblo Acoma N.M.

# 2 Early Development of Stairs

Over time man and animal made paths of the most convenient lanes of passage. On an incline these paths were ramps. Imitating them, early people made earthwork ramps, miniature offspring of hills and mountains. When a log was placed across the ramp, a foothold was created. With such footholds at regular intervals the ramp could be steeper and constructed in less space. When the earth between the logs was leveled off, it became a stairway.

The oldest existing stairway may be the great flights of six thousand granite steps that snake to the top of the most sacred mountain of Tai Shan in China, located in Shantung, a northeastern maritime province. In China too, along the banks of many rivers, are steps from a design as old as Tai Shan, carved anew in the earth with a shovel every spring. At other spots, ramps with logs lead down to the river, repeating another ancient configuration.

In many areas of the world, man's first crude and simple efforts to create steps, stairs, and ladders have remained unchanged well into the twentieth century. Contemporary primitive people were found living in Stone-Age conditions in the rain forest on Mindanao Island in the Philippines, seeking shelter in natural caves reached by primitive steps, little more than natural rock outcroppings on the cliff side, slightly reshaped for easier climbing.

On western Mindanao Island along the Agusan River, the Manobos, who were once slave-raider pagans, build their houses high in the air on tree trunks, shorn of their tops, accessible only by rudimentary ladders, and in the seaport of Zamboanga the Badjao, Muslim sea-gypsies, live in houses built over the water and connected by unsteady walkways with rickety ladders or precarious steps reaching down to the boats that glide below.

On neighboring Borneo, the roomy, palm-thatched houses are elevated two or three feet and reached by a set of elementary steps; while on Celebes the raised huts are reached by lashed-together wood or bamboo ladders, as are similar houses in Malaysia and on the South Sea islands.

Stilt houses and raised houses can be found among the native tribes along the rivers of every South American country; in Africa, several jungle tribes still live in huts on stilts reached by primitive ladders, and in the coastal states on the Gulf of Guinea, such as Benin (formerly Dahomey), stilt houses on tall poles dot the beaches, reached by rudimentary ladders.

In the southwestern United States in New Mexico, Acoma Indians have kept their form of building for centuries at their pueblo isolated on a cliff. Their kivas, circular rooms for worship, have access only by ladder through a hole in the roof.

A very early account of a structure that required steps and stairs is one recorded in the Bible: "And they said, Go to, let us build us a city and a tower, whose top may reach unto heaven." (Genesis 11:4) The Tower of Babel was reportedly a seven-story ziggurat, or series of platforms one atop the other, built like a mesa but artificially constructed, with outside stairways and topped with a temple.

Much architecture in early Egypt was devoted to the religious importance of the afterlife. Temples and tombs were

These ladders and steep stairs without railings were photographed in 1885 at Sky City, the ancestral home of the Acoma, one of the seven Pueblo Indian tribes. The Acoma reservation, located some fifty miles (80 km) from Albuquerque, New Mexico, is claimed to be the oldest inhabited settlement in North America. The double ladder in the center leads to a ceremonial kiva.

The ziggurat of Ur in Mesopotamia, already old when it was remodeled (c. 2125–2025), may have been much like the biblical Tower of Babel. Substantial remains of ziggurats on many sites provide information about their form, material, and details.

Without benefit of later archaeological discoveries, Pieter Brueghel the Elder (1525–69) in his painting of the Tower of Babel, depicted a ziggurat that conformed to the imagery of his own time. The original tower was reconstructed during the reign of Hammurabi (1792–50 B.C.) and then again during the reign of Nebuchadnezzar II (605–562 B.C.) whose goal was "to raise up the top that it might rival heaven." It was called Etemenanki, "home of the terrace platform of heaven and earth," and consisted of a series of square platforms 288 feet (88 m) on a side, rising 288 feet in seven terraces with a shrine of blue-enamelled brick atop. On one side of the first stage, two steep stairways rose more than 100 feet (30.5 m) along the face of the wall forming a triangle and meeting in the middle at a landing, from which a third stairway extended straight out to the ground. Crowds climbed the gigantic stone stairways in procession to the first terrace, from which the priests proceeded by secret flights to the peak where the shrine of the god Marduk stood, furnished with a gold couch and table.

massive and lasting, while palaces and residences were transitory, their walls and stairs built of sun-dried brick. In the stone pylons, the great thick towers that introduced the temple, massive stairways were supported by the walls that surrounded them. The steps in tombs and pyramids survive in claustrophobic shafts that lead to underground burial chambers. A memorable event in archaeology occurred in 1922 when Howard Carter found, cut in the rock, sixteen stone steps that led to the sealed door behind which the treasure of Tutankhamen had lain untouched for 3,265 years.

Many early stairways led to water supplies below ground level. Since they were cut into rocky shafts, they have survived. It is still possible to ascend the very steps from the ancient rock-cut watercourse at Gihon Spring that King David ordered his army commander-in-chief to use in order to infiltrate the stronghold of Jebusi and make possible the Hebrew conquest of Jerusalem.

Excavations on the Greek island of Santorini have uncovered the remains of a city called Akrotiri, which belonged to the civilization destroyed in the earthquake of 1500 B.C. that gave rise to the legend of the sunken Atlantis. Fragments of beautifully painted murals revealed the city to have been Minoan. In the ruins are several double stairways, boxed in by stair walls, the two parallel flights separated by a landing and another thick masonry wall.

Persepolis, capital of ancient Persia and built during the reign of Darius I (522–486 B.C.), stands on a terrace, one side of which is reached by a massive and magnificent double stairway leading to the gate of Xerxes. The wall flanking this stairway, like other surviving stairways in the remote palace complex, has beautifully preserved bas-relief figures that seem to march up the stairs. The Greeks were unaware of Persepolis until during the

conquest of Asia (ca. 330 B.C.) Alexander the Great plundered the city and burned the palace of Xerxes. But since his army was accompanied by surveyors, engineers, and architects, the knowledge of its magnificent architecture was brought back with him.

In early Greece, stairs were neither monumental nor of much importance; interior ones were modest and utilitarian, simply giving access to galleries above. Temples were approached by winding paths that were simple and picturesque by intention.

Crowning the hill of the Acropolis at Athens, the Parthenon was the chief temple of the Greek goddess Athena. Built by the architects Ictinus and Callicrates under the supervision of the sculptor Phidias, work on the temple was begun in 447 B.C. and completed in 438 B.C., with work on the exterior carvings and decoration of the building continuing for six more years. The temple stands on a crepidoma, or stepped platform of three risers that are double the height of normal stairs and with treads double the depth.

In the post-Alexandrian Hellenistic period (323 B.C.–A.D. 300) stairs took on importance and monumentality, an Asiatic influence from Alexander's conquests. The great Altar to Zeus, built at Pergamon in the first century B.C. to commemorate the victory of Attalus I over the Gauls, was distinguished by its monumental steps and its story-high sculptural frieze depicting a battle between the gods and giants. Pergamon, an ancient Greek city built on an isolated hill near the Aegean Sea in what is now Turkey, was excavated beginning in 1878 under the auspices of the Berlin Museum.

The Roman architectural period (300 B.C.–A.D. 365) borrowed building forms from both the Greeks and the Etruscans, early inhabitants of west-central Italy. The Etruscan architectural era (750–100 B.C.) is noted for its development of arches and

"Space, and the twelve clean winds of heaven,
And this sharp exultation, like a cry after the
slow six thousand steps of climbing! This
is Tai Shan, the beautiful, the most holy."

Eunice Tietjens,
*The Most Sacred Mountain*

The peak of Tai Shan towers 5,060 feet (1,542 m)
above the plain of the Yellow River, and the path
that leads to the top culminates in great, soaring
flights of massive granite steps, washed smooth by
wind and rain and the countless footsteps of
pilgrims, Chinese worshippers who toiled up the
rocky steps seeking their god. The stairway has
been consecrated by the footsteps of Confucius
(551–479 B.C.), who was a native of the province,
and who climbed the 6,000 steps to stand on
the holy peak beside the Altar of Heaven. To see the
dawn from the top is said to confer immortality.
The treads of this immense stairway are shallow, so
today's Western visitors find it necessary to watch
every step when climbing Tai Shan. The last flight
is the steepest.

In the town of Dansalan on Lake Lanao on Mindanao stands this old raised house and sturdy access ladder, rare survivors of a disastrous earthquake. Huts built on stilts are commonplace on Mindanao, even where there is no danger of flooding. Such huts stay cool and are safe from marauding animals. Many houses have floor levels raised well above the ground, some with one whole side of the house, from ground to floor level, equipped with a broad ladder of bamboo lashed together in a sturdy, slanted grid.

thick walls. The Romans, the most magnificent builders of the western world at their time, experimented with new materials and techniques and, no later than the second century B.C., developed concrete whose properties tolerated the increased spans required for the construction of bridges, aqueducts, amphitheaters, baths, basilicas, and large temples, as well as the arches that supported intricate flights of stairs.

Monumental stairs were part of the architectural concept of Roman temples, which were not stepped and surrounded by continuous porches as were the Greek temples, but were raised on high straight podiums with the porch at one end. The best preserved Roman temple is the Maison Carrée (16 B.C.) at Nîmes, France. The 12 foot (3.6 m) high podium is extended to flank the stairs, ending in pedestals that supported large sculptures. Within these extensions the bank of stairs with twenty-one steps fills the remainder of the entrance façade. This configuration is typical of other temples: Fortuna Virilis (40 B.C.), Mars Ultor (14–2 B.C.), and Saturn (A.D. 284) in Rome, and the huge Temple of Jupiter at Baalbek, in modern Lebanon, with access steps running the full width of 164 feet (50 m) except for flanking pedestals.

Residential stairways were typically simple, supported by surrounding walls, but Roman construction techniques allowed buildings several stories high. Ruins of apartment blocks can still be seen in Ostia, Rome's ancient harbor. Straight flight and dogleg stairs led from entrances on the street beside the shop front openings to residences above. Intricate configurations of stairs and landings were later developed, such as the elaborate but practical entry and exit stairs to the Colosseum (A.D. 80).

The Romans also found that stairs could be turned around a central core to make a spiral staircase. A marble model of Rome (A.D. 205) shows separate stair towers in an apartment house courtyard. The spiral staircase was an important part of victory columns, the most famous of which is Trajan's Column in Rome (A.D. 113). It is 115 feet (35 m) high, a Doric column built entirely of marble with a spiralling bas-relief band illustrating Trajan's victories.

While the Roman empire dominated Europe, the Chinese empire cast a long shadow in Asia, exerting its influence in cultural and architectural style. Chinese architecture, which shows Mesopotamian influences in the use of arch and vault, has characteristic roof detailing and majestic staircases. The prominence of stairways in Chinese architecture is evident in the fifteenth-century Forbidden City in Beijing, which has numerous stone stairways with massive balustrades.

Concurrently, great civilizations flourished in the Americas, isolated from European and Asian influences. The Aztec, Mayan, Toltec, and Inca civilizations left pyramids and temples, whose designs and function are mysterious and magnificent. These structures were reached by many wide and often excessively steep staircases for both access and ceremonial purposes. Sometimes climbing all four sides of a structure from base to top, stairs are the dominant features of the architecture, as they are on the impressive pyramids at Chichén Itzá (c. A.D. 1200).

Civilizations isolated from one another by oceans, mountains, or great geographical distances and by time can still be expected to respond to the need to gain access to heights in much the same manner, using available materials. The history of architecture shows us that they have indeed done so.

In Israel the winding stairway hugging the wall of the shaft of the great pool of the Gibeon water system was dug before the tenth century B.C. It served as a cistern until a tunnel was added and the stairs continued down to the water table. The steps and a balustradelike protective wall were carved into the bedrock.

Primitive rock stairs carved on a trail in Bandelier National Monument, New Mexico, lead to pre-Columbian Tsankawi and Tyvonyi ruins. These crude steps can be no different in form and execution than those of civilizations older than they.

On the coast of Tunisia in North Africa, facing the Mediterranean near the town of Gabes, three thousand Ghouras live in old cave homes reached by crude footholds carved into the rock. The area was an ancient Barbary state under the suzerainty of Turkey. The Berbers, driven underground by Arab invaders, found the climate of the cave homes so pleasant compared to the scorching heat above ground that they elected to remain there into modern times.

At Persepolis eight grand staircases lead to the Apadana, or ceremonial audience hall, of Darius I; on this one a procession of the Ten Thousand Immortals pace the climbers of the stairs, thus making the retaining wall visually more important than the stairs themselves. Persepolis stands on an immense limestone platform about nine hundred feet (275 m) by fifteen hundred feet (457 m) in dimension and up to fifty feet (15 m) above the plain. It was built by Darius in the fourth century B.C. to exalt the mighty Persian kings and honor the two rulers before him, who during thirty years of conquest had brought Babylonia, Lydia, Syria, Palestine, northern Arabia, and the Nile Valley under Persian control.

This Minoan stairway, destroyed in an earthquake in 1500 B.C., is being excavated on the island of Santorini. The surviving flight of stairs was crushed when the building surrounding it collapsed. Early stairways were most often built inside walls or between two walls to take advantage of earthwork support.

TOP RIGHT
The Parthenon, the most famous Greek temple, crowns the Acropolis in Athens. Its Doric columns stand without a base directly on the crepidoma, a three-stepped platform. Each step is 20 in. (50 cm) high and 28 in. (71 cm) deep, too steep to ascend in comfort. Intermediate steps in the form of blocks were provided on the east and west ends.

The foundations remain on the hill at Pergamon, but the great Altar of Zeus with its monumental stairway and sculptural frieze, a masterpiece of Hellenistic art, have been removed to a museum in East Berlin and reconstructed. Some of the heroic figures seem to have escaped the battle between the gods and giants to stumble up the stairs.

Only by climbing six hundred rough stone steps can one reach the small primitive monastery of Great Skelling atop a bleak little island in County Kerry, Ireland. Built in the sixth century A.D., it was founded by a holy man called Saint Finian. Through the centuries the monks inhabiting the crude beehive-shaped rock huts of the retreat were kept safe from marauding Norsemen, discouraged by the forbidding climb of the primitive and precipitous steps. The last monk abandoned the tiny monastery in the twelfth century, leaving it to nesting sea birds.

Three thousand steps link the five square miles (13 km²) of Machu Picchu, an Inca city of terraces and houses, temples and citadels. High in the Andes of Peru, along a saddle between two steep peaks, the site escaped detection until 1911, when Hiram Bingham came upon magnificent stone terraces seven thousand feet (2133 m) above the Urubamba River. Another three thousand feet (915 m) up the mountainside he reached the deserted city, moss-covered and overrun by the jungle. The remarkable architecture of Machu Picchu is built with huge blocks of stone fitted so closely together, without mortar, that a knifeblade cannot be inserted between them, astounding precision with primitive tools. This beautiful city, linked together with stone stairs, is believed to have been occupied around 1500, the late Inca period, just before the Spanish conquest.

Chichén Itzá, dating from the sixth century A.D. and located in northern Yucatan, Mexico, was the largest, mightiest, and most beautiful of the Mayan cities. This building called the Caracol—named from the Spanish word for snail, because of the winding internal staircase—was reached by a series of broad steps. It was built during the later Mayan-Toltec period and used as an observatory, to record astronomical evidence verifying the accuracy of the Mayan calendar.

OPPOSITE
View of ceremonial buildings and stairways in the Mayan city of Tikal, Guatemala, dated A.D. 292. The tallest stairways at Tikal have a slope of 60 degrees with risers taller than the treads are deep, which symbolizes the need to toil to get closer to the gods. The main structures are truncated pyramids, surmounted by thick-walled sanctuaries where the priests performed secret rituals.

# 3 Stairway Material

The materials available to construct steps and stairs were at first limited to stone, wood, earth, and brick. In the Sumerian city of Ur, which flourished in the thirty-fifth century B.C., bricks made of sun-dried mud and clay were commonly used. By the third millennium B.C. the kiln had been invented, and clay bricks could be fired and made stronger and more durable for use in structures including stairs, treads, and risers.

An early form of cement was used by the Romans more than two thousand years ago, but structural concrete, as we know it today, was developed in the early nineteenth century. The invention of an artificial cement called portland cement made possible the manufacture of a stronger, more durable concrete. By the end of the nineteenth century, concrete was reinforced with steel and greater stair spans and cantilevered steps were possible.

Concrete, and especially brick, are stairway materials today most commonly used outdoors. Concrete can be poured to conform to any stairway shape and configuration and can be studded with pebbles or pitted with salt to provide both ornamentation and rough surface safety. Bricks are by their shape and rich color both ornamental and easy to form into specific designs of treads and risers. And like concrete, they are available in many finishes: plain, wire cut, scored, roughened, sand or water struck, or burned in the firing to produce color variations.

Wrought iron, tougher and harder than bronze, also appeared in Asia Minor in the second millennium B.C., but remained of secondary importance in construction until the development of improved techniques for casting in the seventeenth and eighteenth centuries in Europe. Steel, a toughened and hardened iron, was developed in the nineteenth century and quickly replaced wrought and cast iron as a construction material where strength and durability were needed.

When other materials such as nonferrous metals and alloys, plastic, and fiberglass became obtainable, they permitted more sophisticated design and construction of stairways. These synthetic construction materials, developed during the late nineteenth and early twentieth centuries, allowed more flexible solutions to the restrictions of space and weight, so that stairways that were both functional and aesthetically pleasing could be designed.

*Plastic* is derived from a Greek term *plastikos*, meaning to form, and plastics can easily be formed into any desired shape by heating, milling, molding, or similar processes. The material is light in weight while still being rigid and tough, and those used in construction are hard and durable while easily machinable. Plastics can be manufactured in any color or completely transparent. The first plastic made, Parkesine (later renamed Xylonite), was invented by the British chemist Alexander Parkes in 1862, but only decades later had the material been refined so it could be used in construction.

Fiberglass, a material related to plastics, became available for stairway construction in the present century. Glass fibers have been molded into rigid shapes to form steps, stringers, and carriages, and they are also used to reinforce plastics. Plastic and fiberglass are materials that lend themselves to fluid contours in stairway designs and can be used alone or in various combinations. Materials technology has become so advanced that creativity is limited only by the imagination of the designer.

Assigned to create a nonferrous staircase for the Science Museum in London, which had to be both functional and beautiful, sculptor Michael Black chose aluminum. Tread and baluster are cast as one and threaded on a steel post.

TOP LEFT AND RIGHT
Blocks of stone form massive stairways that connect streets in the Umbrian hill town of Assisi, where Saint Francis preached his affectionate reverence for all living things.

In the Deer Park outside Copenhagen, an edge of stone blocks holds an earthen tread into which cobblestones have been set. A fine moss is encouraged to grow between the stones, and the low rise is made more visible by contrasting stone colors.

Natural stones and tamped-down earth form the risers and treads of this picturesque sylvan stairway that winds through autumn woods in Texas Falls, Vermont.

Top Left
Bricks set in patterns and bordered with stone lead up the hill at Caprarola, to the retreat of the Farnese family. The palace near Viterbo, Italy, was built around 1620 following plans left by the architect Vignola at his death in 1573.

Pebbles set in a pattern and bordered in bull-nosed stone form treads at Villa Garzoni in the hills north of Lucca, Italy.

OPPOSITE
TOP LEFT
Steps of precisely hewn granite blocks lead in uniform symmetry to the wooden deck surrounding a Japanese shrine.

CENTER
In contrast, these Japanese garden steps made of natural boulders and rocks are carefully arranged to appear random and artless.

BOTTOM
Bricks form treads and risers, landings and walls for the entry of a residence in Beverly Hills, California.

RIGHT
Where the mountains were too steep to scale, Pueblo Indians of the southwestern United States chiseled crude steps into the face of the cliff.

A skeleton of structural steel makes possible this sweep of concrete stairs, cast in place before the house was enclosed. The freestanding stairway, designed by architect Lyman Ennis, is supported only on the floor at its foot and does not touch the floor above.

Designer Robert Ross used polished stainless steel for the steps of this shiny stairway and burnished brass for the handrail, creating an image of reflected brilliance at this restaurant in Los Angeles.

The impressive entrance hall to the Marble House in Newport, Rhode Island, is a prime example of marble used in building a staircase. Many famous staircases are made of marble or travertine, materials favored for stairway construction.

This spectacular black marble staircase, designed by Bruce Bryant for Marble Works, Los Angeles, seems transformed into a double staircase at the top, but it is an illusion created by the adjoining mirrored wall.

Old railroad ties serve as both treads and risers of these garden steps.

The rustic staircase of natural logs and tree limbs still rises from the lobby of McDonald Lodge in Glacier Park, Montana, as it did in this photograph from 1920.

The manufacturer of this stair tower, Trip-Trap of Hadsund, Denmark, calls it a Roman tower. Made of pine from Lapland in Norway and Västerbotten in Sweden, it stands assembled in the factory, ready for delivery. Each tread extends from the newel and is pegged through a facet in the tower wall. The designer is Jens Quistgaard.

Interlocking slabs of wood form treads and risers for an intricate, self-supporting stairway in the home of architect Raymond Kappe.

Wood is the material most commonly used in stairway building. This staircase in San Francisco, built by the Durney brothers, is a particularly rich example of its use.

Stair sculptors Jody and Chris Norskog laminated the gracefully twisted single stringer of this staircase from forty-two plies of $5/16$ in. (.8 cm) Honduras mahogany, applied one ply per day. The stringer was carved and notched to hold the treads. The handrail was made of metal piping and a laminated wood rail for which the stair itself was used as a bending form.

This staircase with its multicolored and multipatterned tiled risers stands in the courtyard of a California apartment house.

Treads, newel, balusters, and handrail are made of Lucite in this spiral staircase.

BOTTOM RIGHT
Transparent Lucite treads and open risers offer a view of the room below in an Albuquerque residence designed by architect Bart Prince.

Like an incomplete Möbius strip, the slender, glass-balustraded stairway from the offices above comes to rest on the banking floor of the Allied Bank in Houston, Texas, now the First Interstate Bank, housed in a seventy-one story, blue-green glass tower. The interiors and the unusual stairway were designed by Gensler Associates.

The original larger model of this cast-iron stairway, twenty feet (6 m) in height and six and a half feet (2 m) in diameter, was installed in a paper mill in 1890 in Ottawa, Canada. It was purchased and removed from the mill by Steptoe and Wife Antiques, who adapted it to a spiral five feet (1.5 m) in diameter, which they make available in parts of cast iron and brass.

# 4
# Treads and Risers

While the height of a vertical riser is limited by the capacity of humans to step up and therefore should be no more than twelve inches (30.5 cm), the horizontal tread is not governed by such limitations. The depth of the tread may range from one to several feet, yet still define a stairway. The breadth of each tread can vary from the width of a man's foot, as it is in some stairs hewn into the rock in Africa or in the Andes, to the 282 foot (86 m) wide sweep of the stairway to the Sydney Opera House.

A tread may be oblong or semicircular in shape, rectangular or square; a triangular wedge anchored to a central newel post, or a slab cantilevered from a wall. Some treads are round or irregularly shaped, solid or open-grated, skid-proofed with rubber tread covers or metal plank grating. Whether built, prefabricated for on-site assembly, or adapted to a natural formation, treads may be opaque or translucent, iridescent, or illuminated in a great variety of ways. The riser can be

constructed or cast, laminated or carved, separately or as an integral part of the entire step. Risers offer great decorative possibilities—to be ornamented with patterns in tile, filigree, appliqué, or simple paint to delight the ascending eye. Or, since it is really only the distance between two treads, the riser may be nonexistent, merely an open space. The stairs can be covered with carpeting or runners held in place by plain or ornamented stair-rods, painted and decorated in diverse fashions.

Medieval builders correctly observed that when ascending or descending a stairway only one foot at a time rests on any given tread. Therefore they designed a tread that did not stretch the full width of the stair, the alternating-tread concept. Stepping from tread to tread on a conventional stairway, the foot must travel over the unused and therefore unnecessary portion of the tread, which actually becomes an obstacle. The alternating-step concept provides a separate step for each foot, eliminating the waste of material,

OPPOSITE
In Caltagirone, Sicily, a flourishing inland town and a pottery center, a great broad stair flight faced with brightly patterned tiles rises from the piazza.

Incised into the top tread of a short flight of stairs down to a craft shop in Copenhagen, this mustachioed granite greeter beams his welcome.

space, and motion inherent in the full-width tread. The unnecessary half of the tread is left open, and each foot steps straight through the space that in the conventional system it must arc over. Since each tread is deeper, filling the space voided by the step above, each foot has access to a larger tread area than on a conventional stairway.

The alternating-tread stairway also saves floor space, important in such situations as industrial plants, because it can be constructed at a steeper angle while still providing usable tread area comparable to a conventional stairway. Since the alternating-tread stairway can be constructed with a 70-degree pitch, as opposed to a conventional stairway, which must be less than 50 degrees, up to half of the floor space it occupies can be eliminated.

Whether ascending or descending the alternating-tread stairway, the body's center of gravity remains directly over the feet, another significant advantage of the design concept. A distinct disadvantage, which has limited its use, is that people cannot meet and pass on this type of stairway, so it can be used only by people going in the same direction. The conventional configuration is thus more flexible.

Top
**On wintery stairs at Big Bear, California, the open risers are almost obscured by icicles.**

**Like the paddles of a windmill the triangular wedges of the wire-mesh treads of a spiral staircase swirl into the sky.**

The shadowy patterns of a stairway in Silver Mill, which is now a ghost town at Elkhorn, Montana, recall a poem by Hughes Mearns, American writer and educator (1878–1965):

> As I was going up the stair,
> I met a man who wasn't there.
> He wasn't there again today,
> I wish, I wish he'd go away.
> "The Psychold"

TOP
As these steps in the Roman amphitheater in Fiesole suggest, treads and risers have changed little through the ages. Situated on a hill overlooking Florence and the Arno River, the theater dates from the first century B.C. The well-preserved ruins were excavated in 1873.

BOTTOM
These garden steps of precast concrete slabs form an intriguing herringbone pattern on a secluded path.

The combination of stairs and ramping, which the architect calls a "stramp," was designed for a complex in Vancouver, British Columbia, by Arthur Erickson, Architects, to meet handicap requirements.

Long flights of steps, their ends cantilevered, lead ▷ to the top of the 25 foot (7.5 m) high city walls of this historic French city. The little seaport of Aigues-Mortes, located in the marshes of the Rhône River delta west of Marseilles, was built by King Louis IX, who in 1248 and 1270 embarked from its port on his two crusades. Its thirteenth-century ramparts, fortifications, and stairways are among the best preserved in Europe.

Each riser of the unpainted wood steps to the main shrine at Meiji Jingu in Tokyo, which holds the tombs of Emperor Meiji and the Empress Dowager Shoken, has an ornate brass plaque, which leads the eye to the richly ornamented doors.

The Temple of Heaven in Beijing was erected in 1420. Ornate white marble stairs lead to the temple with its triple roof of blue tiles. The emperor in his sedan chair was carried over the richly carved ramp between the stair flights.

In the Doge's Palace, Venice, the famous Giants' Staircase (1485–89), flanked by Mars and Neptune, is ornamented with applied lead designs in different patterns on each riser.

The stairway treads of New York City's Palladium, by architects Arata Isozaki & Associates, dazzle with illuminated discs.

The metal-grate treads on these steps from the street to an apartment house are well suited to the climate of Copenhagen. Open grating allows snow from shoes and boots to pass through instead of building up on the tread.

This entry stairway to a house in Georgetown, Washington, D.C., is assembled of prefabricated cast-iron parts including filigrees of stars and scrolls in its open risers.

Each tread, riser, and side panel of this Victorian-inspired cast-iron stairway by Steptoe and Wife is a separate casting for on-site assembly.

The marble treads and landings of the ornamental iron staircase at the Bradbury Building in Los Angeles are opaque when viewed while ascending the stairs, but become translucent when seen from below because of light flooding the interior court from the skylight above.

Using little more floor space than that taken by a ladder, this split-tread stairway, by Lapeyre Stair in New Orleans, offers comfort and safety in an industrial setting where space is at a premium.

Wooden alternating-tread stairs with a central supporting rail.

In the remodeled town house of Chicago architect Peter Landon, the top of the stairs to the attic work space had to be located in the center of the eighteen foot (5.5 m) wide house, where the roof peak afforded extra room. This alternating-tread stairway reaches a full story, using minimal space.

Each tread, a single slab of wood, cantilevers beyond its supporting stringer to form an unusual open-riser staircase in the entry hall of a residence by architect J. R. Davidson.

Sculptor Tom Luckey created this stairway with its unique treads for a family in Vermont. When a lever is pulled, the treads turn into a ramp, and the stairway becomes a slide for the kids. Luckey most enjoys watching his stairway when it is in transition: Now it's a stairway, now it is not.

# 5 Banisters and Balustrades

Ascending or descending a stairway is a series of perilous maneuvers. On each tread during the ascent the entire weight of the body is balanced momentarily on one foot, while the other foot finds a hold on the next tread. The balance is then transferred to the leading foot, while the body is hauled up the height of the riser. In descending, the body—balanced on one foot—is thrust out over the void, while the leading foot finds its hold on the tread below, transferring the balance and stopping the incipient fall. The risk of this choreography is much reduced by the use of a handrail. Modern concepts of safety require continuous handrails on stairways so that the hand need not leave the rail during the entire ascent or descent and balusters that are spaced close enough so that small children cannot squeeze through. Balustrades provide not only handholds but protection from falling off the precipitous sides of flights of stairs. A primitive form of handhold is carved into the rock in Chaco Canyon in the American Southwest beside gouged-out steps, almost ladder steep.

The earliest interior stairways were enclosed on either side by supporting walls, which provided protection if not a handhold. The early exterior stairs usually rose along a building wall and were supported on the open side by a lower wall often extending hip high above the treads like a parapet wall and thus providing protection and railing.

Early examples of such balustrade configurations can be found in Mesopotamian architecture, and in the House of the Beautiful Courtyard in Herculaneum, where the protective wall has a rounded top serving as a comfortable railing. But during the Renaissance architects developed a balustrade without precedent in the Western world, and that form defining balustrades persists to this day.

*Baluster*, a pillar supporting a handrail, derives from the Italian *balaustra*, because of the resemblance of the pillar to the double curving calyx tube of the wild pomegranate flower, the *balausto*. Renaissance balusters were molded, usually round, with a base and a capital and a vase shape like the pomegranate flower in between. The word *baluster* was corrupted already in the seventeenth century to *banister*.

OPPOSITE
**Old houses on Nantucket Island off the New England coast have a hollow space in the newel post covered by a wooden button. When the mortgage on the house was paid off, the mortgage papers were burned and the ashes placed in the newel post along with a newly minted coin to denote the year. At that point the wooden button was often replaced by an ivory one, logically called the mortgage button.**

◁ **Classic vase-shaped forms define the balustrade of this stairway leading to the upper plaza of the Church of San Francisco in Assisi, Italy.**

The massive construction of these stair railings in
the Forbidden City in Beijing give the effect of
battlements. Many versions of these railings are to
be seen in this immense walled compound of
palaces and courtyards that was the heart of China
and the home of its emperors from 1421 to 1911.

Splendid golden dragons arch elaborately carved
backs to fashion a formidable handrail, capping the
simple white walls that enclose this staircase in
Thailand.

Iron balustrades with gilded details adorn the stairs from the upper garden to the garden drawing room of the Grand Trianon at Versailles.

The monumental staircase of the Bethesda Terrace in New York's Central Park was added in 1873. It was designed by Calvert Vaux, one of the original designers of the park in 1857, and Jacob Wrey Mould. As early as 1890 the intricate carvings on the finely grained sandstone began to show wear. Today these carved panels and handrails on the closed stringers of the stairway, as well as the pillars, columns, and finials, are being restored.

In this 1921 photograph of stairs in Chaco Canyon, New Mexico, gouged-out handholds clearly can be seen paralleling the steep stairs to the mesa like two dotted lines.

<small>Opposite</small>
Students at the Hampton Institute in Virginia, founded by General Samuel Chapman Armstrong for the education of young blacks only recently freed from slavery, are working on the banister at the treasurer's residence. In 1899, the second director of the institute commissioned the prominent photographer Frances Benjamin Johnston to take photographs that show the progress made by the institution in creating a new life for its charges.

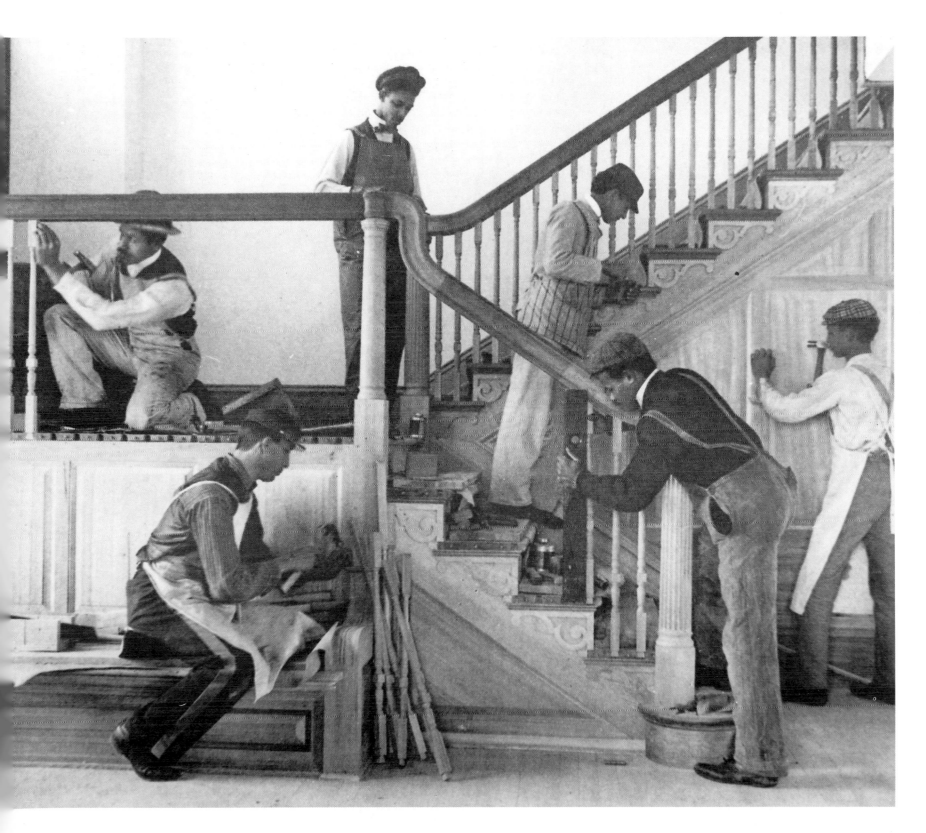

This staircase at Buda Castle in Budapest has a banister built as an integral part of the wall around which it curves, with an open channel that serves to drain rainwater.

Top Right
The spectacular water chain at Villa Lante above Bagnaia, Italy, is channeled through the balustrades and flows into a pool. In this unusual design, the water collects in the flat areas of the balustrade before spilling down to the next level, creating a stairway lively with sound and motion.

These balustrades of an open-air stairway in Yugoslavia have intricately carved banister panels.

Glazed blue-and-white balusters support tiled handrails on bridges and stairs in Seville's Plaza de España in Maria Luisa Park.

The resplendent and opulent old landmark hotel,
the Jefferson Sheraton in Richmond, Virginia, has
undergone a complete restoration under the
direction of architect Brad Elias. The restored grand
staircase with its elaborate cast-metal balustrades
and newels once again descends majestically
into the colonnaded rotunda of the Palm Court.

RIGHT
Derby House, the oldest brick house in Salem,
Massachusetts, was built in 1762 and contains a
staircase with delicately carved balusters and newel
posts, which bear witness to the skill of early Salem
craftsmen.

OPPOSITE
Ornate newel post in a Los Angeles Victorian
residence designed by architect Joseph Cather
Newsom around 1890.

RIGHT
This balustrade incorporates a parade of bronze figures by sculptor Robert Graham. A pair of Graham sculptures flanks the stairway in this entry hall to a mid-Manhattan penthouse designed by Richard Ohrbach and Lynn Jacobsen.

TOP
A similar conceit of permanent climbers appears on the stairway wall of this narrow staircase to a small children's museum in Copenhagen, where a colorful mural of children climbs the stairs. And two and a half millennia before, on the protective wall of a stairway in ancient Persepolis, bodyguards of the empire were carved in bas-relief mounting the steps. The cylindrical headgear with tight pleats identify them as Persians.

In Saint Stephen's Cathedral, established in 1147 in Vienna, the stone railing that leads to the pulpit is adorned with a procession of squat toads and frogs, symbolizing the wicked. They crawl up the hand-rail to be rebuffed at the top by a barking dog.

**TOP**
This staircase with its harplike balustrade stands in
a cottage on Coronado Island in San Diego. It was
designed by architect Irving Gill and built in 1898.
Ninety years later, when architect Dale St. Denis
remodeled the house, all the natural woodwork
including the harp balustrade was painted white.

**BOTTOM**
Nylon with a continuous steel core for strength is
the material used in these banisters, which hold
clear, solid glass panels. The color is infused
throughout the nylon, so the banisters, manufactured by HEWI, suffer no deterioration in brilliance,
even after years of constant use.

The design based on the Japanese "lifting cloud" motif of this wooden balustrade, built in 1908 for Mr. and Mrs. David Gamble in Pasadena, California, displays the characteristic craftsmanship of architects Henry and Charles Greene.

OPPOSITE
In a beach house designed by architect Brad Elias, a handcarved oak stairway grows like a tree from green floor tiles, molded like turf around its roots. A branch growing downward from the tree-limb balusters becomes a handrail for the stairs below. Safety and building department codes are satisfied by the continuous handrail snaking along the wall like a vine.

# 6
# Exterior Stairways

Exterior steps and stairways are of lower and broader proportions than interior stairs because the stride is more vigorous and expansive outdoors than indoors. The materials for exterior stairs are limited since they must endure rain, ice, and snow and tolerate the scorching sun. Stone is therefore an excellent and lasting building material for exterior stairways, whether natural stones, selected for their flatness, size, and shape, or hewn granite or marble. Concrete is one of the most often used stairway materials. Brick and tile also survive well over time. In many archaeological digs stairs have been found relatively intact when the buildings have turned to rubble around them, and in the most destructive fires of our day, steps and stairways have been the last structures left standing.

Exterior stairs fall into two main categories: those that stand free and independent from any structures and those that provide access to buildings and are attached to them. The unattached stairway may be a simple, utilitarian access to a public space—a park, beach, plaza, or streetscape. It can be a grand stairway of heroic proportions, a few plain steps, or the street itself.

In hill towns throughout the world, the slope of streets is often so steep that they must give way to stairs. These stairs, which picturesquely thread their way between buildings to the tops of the hills, become thoroughfares to shops and residences, public meeting places, and little private courts. On the stairway streets in the towns and villages that ring the Mediterranean, there are often offshoots of other stairs that lead to individual houses along the way creating a labyrinth of stairs. Other open spaces may be little landings just big enough for a couple of chairs and the gossip of the day.

The greatest of the Mediterranean hill towns is Rome and many of its thoroughfares are long stairways. The city has five great stairways that lead up or down to the Capitol alone. The most imposing of them is the steep marble stairway of thirteen flights totaling 124 steps to the Church of Santa Maria in Aracoeli, which once provided the only access to the lower part of Rome. It was built in 1348 using not only inspiration from the Romans, but steps taken from the Roman Temple of Serapis.

In about 1546 Michelangelo planned the reconstruction of the Capitol in Rome along symmetrical lines. The spine of his design is the long, broad, solidly balustraded stairway with its shallow risers and deep ramped treads that rises gradually from the streets below to the top of one of Rome's famed hills, next to the steep steps to the Church of Santa Maria in Aracoeli. The greatest and best known of Rome's stairs is Scala di Spagna, the Spanish Steps. Breathtakingly beautiful, it is interrupted midway by a broad landing.

Many cultures share the notion that anything elevated must be important. Heaven is high: rulers are seated on high, exalted places; the mighty are not just mighty, they are also high; temples, churches, and shrines are often on top of hills. The grand staircases at places of prominence are intended to awe, to heighten anticipation, and sometimes to inspire reverence, even fear.

The visitor to the Forbidden City in Beijing, which was once the exclusive domain of the emperors of China, cannot but feel overwhelmed moving between

This tall, 60 degree–steep stairway in Uxmal, Mexico, leads to the so-called Magician's House. Uxmal, once the center of the Mayan New Empire, was founded in 987 and abandoned in 1441. It contains some of the finest examples of Mayan architectural renaissance mainly rendered in limestone. Under the steep steps is a Mayan arch, not unlike that developed by the Romans.

The fabled light of Venice falls on the arch-supported stairway from the courtyard to the museum dedicated to the prolific Italian dramatist Carlo Goldoni (1707–93). This charming small museum was once the house of Goldoni, who virtually replaced the established Italian comedy of stock, masked figures and predictable farce with spontaneity and tightly constructed plots to become the founder of Italian realistic comedy.

OPPOSITE

The broad balustraded stairs spilling down from the façade of the cathedral of Saint Paul are a landmark and gathering place in Macao, a city settled in 1513 by the Portuguese and officially ceded to its king in 1557. Construction of Saint Paul's began in 1602 under Jesuits assisted by Japanese Christians, who had fled religious persecution in Nagasaki. In 1835 the church burned to the ground, leaving only its ornate façade and the broad stairs leading up to its plaza.

**Reminiscent of early Roman construction, this arched stone stairway at a small hotel on Bequai Island in the Caribbean was designed by architect Raymond Crites.**

the massive, confining balustrades when climbing the great marble stairways to the terraces. Often the building to be reached cannot fully be seen from the stairfoot, adding a touch of mystery, even apprehension, to the ascent. Just outside Beijing stands the magnificent Temple of Heaven, crowning a steep-sided terrace. From the stairs below, little of the temple, where Ming rulers came to make sacrifice to the deity who empowered their dynasty, can be seen. Even the emperor must have felt some awe or apprehension when he was carried up the steps to the temple, which would seem to rise up little by little, revealing its imposing splendor to him slowly as he reached the top.

In ascending Mayan and Inca temples, the structure atop the pyramid is also obscured from the foot of the stairs. Not only is climbing the very high risers and narrow treads exhausting, but the fear of the unseen and unknown at the top must take its toll. The descent on such stairs is even more difficult, but for some there was no descent at all—their destination was the sacrificial altar high above.

Attached stairways providing access to buildings are often no less impressive and awe-inspiring than those that are independent of them. Many public buildings—capitols and courts, churches and temples, theaters and libraries—are reached by monumental grand stairways. Such stairways introduce a quality of theater: choirs and choruses arrange themselves on them, rallies are staged on them, and they are particularly well suited for ceremonies and public speaking.

Exterior stairways throughout the world that have captured special architectural or popular interest would include the set of six imposing flights of stairs at Sans Souci in Potsdam. Sans Souci, French for "without care," was built by the Prussian warrior king, Frederick the Great during 1745–48, and is one of the world's greatest pleasure palaces. The principal

architect, Georg Wenzeslaus von Knobelsdorf (1699–1754), worked closely from sketches made by the king himself. The wide stairways lead from the Marble Hall in the south façade of the palace down a number of terraces to the garden below. On each terrace grow grapevines and flowers in narrow spaces behind sheltering glass.

In the city of Krasnador in Russia a huge expanse of stairs that form all four sides of an enormous rectangular platform, built like a ziggurat, gives access to a great modern motion-picture theater. In England, the horseshoe grand staircase of Kedleston Hall near Derby, which leads to the *piano nobile*, the main floor typically containing reception rooms with higher ceilings than the floors above, is considered to be one of the finest exterior designs by the celebrated eighteenth-century British architect, Robert Adam, who is primarily remembered for his interiors.

On a hill three miles southeast of Braga, Portugal, stands the sanctuary of Bom Jesus do Monte, renowned for its spectacular eighteenth-century staircase and visited on Whitsunday by thousands of pilgrims. The wide stairway bordered by solid stone balustrades leads to the most dramatic part, the six stages of steps to the pilgrimage church itself, flanked with chapels each containing a carved representation of one of the Stations of the Cross. The spectacular effect is heightened by the zigzag plan with the angles accentuated with fountains, statues, and obelisks in granite.

The form of staircases in many villas, palaces, and great houses is closely related to that of grand public staircases. Villa Spina in Palermo, Italy, and Drumlanrig Castle near Thornhill, Scotland, have stone-balustraded horseshoe stairs of a configuration that suggests Fontainebleau; and Schloss Biebrich in Wiesbaden, Germany, has a similar horseshoe staircase,

**Outside the World Trade Center in New York, a sweep of curved, concentric stairs in concave configuration leads to the main entrance of Bankers Trust Plaza.**

TOP LEFT
**At the Prior's Palace in Perugia, Italy, a stack of semicircular slabs of diminishing size forms a convex stairway structure favored by people watchers.**

A brown volcanic stone, typical of the Umbrian hills, forms both a broad flight of stairs and the façade of the beautiful Gothic city hall in Viterbo.

A pyramidal configuration of six steps leads to the upper garden where richly balustraded stairs rise to the garden drawing room of the Grand Trianon. The pink marble palace, designed in 1687 by Jules Hardouin-Mansart, was built in the park of Versailles for Louis XIV. Fallen into disrepair, the palace underwent a thorough restoration beginning in 1962.

but with a gossamer-fine iron balustrade.

Exterior staircases to private residences and other personal quarters from barns to boarding houses may differ in size and use from those in public buildings, but they are otherwise the same in design and purpose. Wherever houses and shelters are constructed, builders have found that it is preferable to raise the level of the floor rather than placing it continuous with the level of the ground on which the shelter stands. In many places the first floor level of a house is raised enough to protect from floods during rainy season or to rise above the snow.

For many people in the world's crowded places, home is a narrow dwelling a short flight of steps up from a narrow street. The stairway at each house is of similar shape and size and forms a pattern: for instance, New York's brownstones and San Francisco's wooden Victorians; the white-washed villages of Greece and Turkey; Mexico's adobes and Italy's hilltown houses.

All across America a Victorian heritage has left wide, open social porches with a few broad front steps up to an area that invites long conversations into a summer night. When bungalows of Japanese inspiration replaced the Victorian

style, the porch was retained but given a somewhat lower perspective with steps centered on it. The ranch house, developed in America during the post–World War II era, sent the art of building front porches and stairs into dormancy, for their concrete slab floors were poured on the ground on the flat building sites available, offering more direct access to the out-of-doors.

In regions of hills and mountains, available flat land was preferred as building sites, but as it became scarce or was needed for farming, buildings or whole villages were located on hills, and today hillside building sites are common.

Heights offer the advantages of views, privacy, and protection, and they provide incentives to build interesting stairways. Old hillside villages are inspiration and models for the new: modern Catalina Island studies Capri, and Ricardo Bofill echoes elements of Spanish hill towns in his stairway designs.

Staircases in today's large public buildings are a secondary means of access because these buildings are serviced by escalators and elevators from the lobby or garage. Stairs are still the main access to private residences, however, and are basically unchanged in importance, function, and shape.

LEFT
**A divided broad stoop leads to a duplex in a row of Victorian houses in San Francisco.**

CENTER
**Identical iron entry stairs in Georgetown, Washington, D.C., are distinguished by individual paint colors.**

RIGHT
**The entry stairway to a narrow, elegant, New York City brownstone is introduced by heavy newel posts.**

◁ In a street of steps in the Italian village of Sanni-
candro, graded stones form a narrow ramp to
accommodate a wheelbarrow.

Top
The stone steps in an old district of Perigueux, on
the river Isle in the Dordogne region of southwestern France, have a gutter carved out of the steps
in the middle of the narrow street that channels
rainwater down the flight of stairs.

Bottom Left
In this Italian hilltown village of Castelvecchio
Calviso, the stairways to the houses, packed
together on the narrow streets, are curved and the
top landings cantilevered to permit a loaded
donkey room to thread its way between them.

This picturesque stair-street, barred to vehicular
traffic, is in the Italian town of Spoleto, northeast of
Rome.

No fallen leaf remains for long on the stone block steps to this shrine in Kyoto.

Flights of stairs connect the stepped platforms of Toksu, the fifteenth-century Palace of Virtuous Longevity, facing the City Hall in Seoul, Korea.

The climb up the steep, narrow stair on the central ▷ tower, or *prang*, of the magnificent Thai monastery, Wat Arun—Temple of the Dawn—leaves the visitor breathless and in awe. The temple stands on the west bank of the Chao Phraya River in Thon Buri, Bangkok's twin city. Construction of the central *prang* and the smaller ones surrounding it was begun in 1809 by King Rama II. The towers are made of brick covered with stucco and decorated with thousands of pieces of multicolored Chinese porcelain and pottery.

From the Square Willette monumental stairways rise toward the gleaming, white Basilique du Sacre Coeur, which stands majestically on the heights of Montmartre, the highest point in Paris. Here, according to legend, the first bishop of Paris and patron saint of France, Saint Denis, was martyred by decapitation in the third century during the persecution of Christians by the Roman emperor Valerian. The church was designed by French architect Paul Abadie, who took his inspiration from the twelfth-century Romanesque church of Saint Front in Perigueux with its five domes. Work was begun in 1876, but Abadie died before the church was completed.

OPPOSITE

The vast ceremonial steps ascending the platform on which the Sydney Opera House stands are 282 feet (86 m) wide. Situated on Bennelong Point, a narrow peninsula, the graceful tile-clad shells that form the roofs of the buildings look like giant barnacles encrusting the landspit, a motif in keeping with the harbor setting. This spectacular complex, which houses not only the opera house but also a theater, concert hall, cinema, and restaurant, was designed by the Danish architect Jørn Utzon in 1973.

The coil of openwork tracery reveals the stair within the tower adorning the pinnacled Milan cathedral. In construction for a century, beginning in 1385, it soars in lacelike intricacy over the city.

TOP RIGHT

These steps with their massive balustrades lead to the Hofburg Palace in Vienna, the sprawling imperial residence where Emperor Franz Joseph lived until his reign ended at his death in 1916. It has undergone several changes and additions since the Habsburgs founded their seat in the thirteenth century. The present palace dates mostly from 1547–52, but the structure grew as the Austro-Hungarian Empire grew, with the latest addition made in 1913, five years before the end of the Habsburg reign.

RIGHT

This simple stone stairway, known as the Dorothy Vernon Stairway at Haddon Hall in Derbyshire, England, has captured public interest because of the romantic legend attached to it. Sir George Vernon, the last of the Vernons to occupy Haddon Hall, was a harsh man, unalterably opposed to his daughter Dorothy's wish to marry young John Manners, son of the Earl of Rutland. At the height of the celebration of her sister's wedding in 1563, Dorothy quietly opened the door at the head of these stone stairs already then covered in moss and lichen, and fled, so legend has it, into the arms of her waiting lover.

The château at Blois in the Loire Valley in France began as a feudal castle and displays typical architectural styles from the thirteenth to the seventeenth centuries. The Francis I façade, dating from 1515–24, with its octagonal staircase tower with stairs that spiral five stories, is a pure Renaissance design.

Through the archway at the top of the long stairway leading to the Castle of Buda above the Danube in Budapest, a statue of Saint Stephen can be glimpsed. The fortress was built on Buda Hill by King Bela IV in the years following the invasion of the Mongols in 1241.

TOP CENTER
Stair-street in the Adriatic seaport of Dubrovnik, a city founded in the seventh century A.D. by Romans fleeing the Slavic sacking of Epidaurus. The old city is a maze of twisting, steep, and narrow streets with many stairs leading to the promenade atop the city walls.

TOP RIGHT
Narrow street of steps in the town of Skanzen, Hungary.

The Metropolitan Elevated Railroad Station, which once stood at 14th Street in New York City, was inspired by Swiss chalet architecture and built after a design by the painter Jasper Cropsey. The structure concealed a double staircase giving access to the trains above. The photograph was taken about 1879.

Many of the over four hundred bridges in Venice are arched high, necessitating steps to cross the two hundred canals and nearly thirty miles of waterways in that city.

The picturesque roofed structure on the façade of the town hall of Rietberg, Germany, outlines the double staircase within.

On Bali, which has remained primarily Hindu, each village temple has a day on which it is afforded special homage, including a colorful procession up the stairway leading to it.

RIGHT
The steps to the Giant Bell at Wat Pho in Bangkok, Thailand.

At Temple Kehen Bangli in Bali, several short flights of steps lead to a platform that serves as an altar, where worshippers can leave the elaborate offerings they have made for the gods.

The stairway that leads to the Buddhist temple of Doi Suthep in Chiang Mai, Thailand, is as colorful as the architecture itself.

Each year during the Thaipusam Festival, Malaysian devotees climb the stairs to the Batu Caves, vast caverns of staggering beauty in a spectacular limestone outcropping that holds the Hindu shrine of Lord Subramaniam. The caves located near Kuala Lumpur, capital of Malaysia, are reached by a stairway of 272 steps.

At the Michelangelo-designed staircase to the Capitol in Rome, here pictured in an etching by Piranesi, two Egyptian lionesses, fashioned into fountains, guard the stairfoot, and the stairhead is flanked by two giant statues of Castor and Pollux standing on massive newel pedestals, each heroic figure holding a magnificent horse. The stairway leads to the Campidoglio Plaza on which stands the superb bronze statue of Marcus Aurelius. On the plaza, centered on the stairway, is the Palazzo Senatorio with a magnificent balustraded double staircase gracing its façade. This central palace is flanked by two other palaces. The façades of all three buildings were designed by Michelangelo, as were the two great stairways rising to higher levels on each side of the plaza.

A second, more gradual and easily climbed stair was provided for the old and the infirm beside the steep main stairway to the Ouro Preto Church above the town of Santa Efigenia, Brazil. The church was built through the efforts of a former slave, an African chieftain who had struck it rich when gold was first discovered in Brazil around 1698.

Michelangelo's double flight of balustraded stairs ▷ from the Palazzo Senatorio down to the Piazza del Campidoglio on which it stands.

According to architect Fred Bassetti, the lighthearted architecture of these intricate stairs and landings at the Federal Building in Seattle presents so intriguing a climb that elevator loads inside the building have lightened considerably.

BOTTOM LEFT
Stairway maze by Dave Phillips challenges the use of stairs.

BOTTOM RIGHT
*Relativity* by Mauritz Cornelius Escher. Courtesy of the Vorpal Galleries, San Francisco and New York.

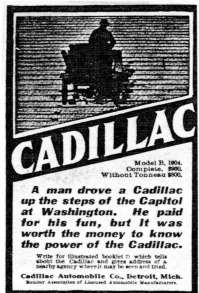

TOP LEFT

The competition for the design of the Capitol
building, the seat of the Congress of the United
States, was won by an East-Indian doctor, William
Thornton, in 1792. Thornton, however, lacked
technical experience, so the runner-up, Stephen
Hallet, had to supervise the construction. George
Washington laid the cornerstone in 1793, and
Congress convened in the newly completed north
wing in November 1800. In 1882 the Capitol
steps were used to demonstrate the versatility of the
latest bicycles.

TOP RIGHT

The steps to the Capitol building have been the
scene for many varied activities: celebrations and
receptions for dignitaries, demonstrations and
political rallies, sightseeing and rendezvous,
publicity stunts, and even a torrid sexual encounter
between a U.S. Congressman and his wife. Here,
they are used as a snow bank for sledding.

◁ In 1904 the steps were featured in a Cadillac ad.

Steps to the channeled and landscaped San Antonio
River, which winds through the downtown area of
San Antonio, Texas.

Typical steps to a white-washed house in a village
in Greece.

A stair-path of 586 deep, ramped treads and shallow ▷
risers snakes its way down the towering cliffs of
Santorini to the water below.

Simple exterior steps lead to the roof of this unusual, white-washed house in southernmost Italy, where many unusual architectural shapes are based on the abundance of limestone rock.

On the wall of a studio in Los Angeles, designed by architect Stephen Ehrlich, the shadows betray the existence of the staircase.

◁ Eight cascades, eight separate villas and their long series of connecting stairways, comprise Ocho Cascadas, a spectacular complex designed by Ed Giddings and located on the coast in Puerto Vallarta, Mexico.

Inhabitants of this modern Hong Kong high rise festoon the stairtower of the building with banner-like laundry on bamboo poles. The occupants still prefer stairs to elevators.

La Muralla Roja in La Manzanera, a residential resort complex designed by Ricardo Bofill, 1969–83, is a shocking pink building standing on a cliff in Alicante, Spain. The stairs with their sawtoothed balustrades are as playful as children's building blocks. With evident links to the symbolism of Postmodern architecture and to Gaudí, Bofill and his colleagues shock and delight critics in their search for a new vocabulary of urban form.

The international insurance firm, Lloyd's of London, has come a long way since the company began in a small seventeenth-century coffeehouse. Their new quarters, a fourteen-story high rise designed by architect Richard Rogers, was completed in 1986. The floors are accessed from six gleaming, stainless-steel towers, each structurally independent and incorporating both a staircase and elevators.

On a flat site subject to flooding, building construction requires unconventional measures. In this vacation house designed by Mies van der Rohe for Dr. Edith Farnsworth and completed in 1950, two slabs, hovering in space, suspended on eight **H**-beams, form floor and ceiling. Another travertine-paved slab floats as a deck between the floor slab and the ground, with a short flight of steps leading from the deck to the living space. The unchanged site is touched only by the supporting beams and the slender, almost unseen supports of the travertine slabs that are the stair treads to the deck.

Right

Slabs of pebbled concrete are placed separately up the hillside to form treads and risers of this stairway, which connects the parking area with the house above, designed by Richard Neutra.

Opposite
Left

The Haliburton house has been a landmark on a high ridge in the hills south of Laguna Beach, California, since 1937. Because of the inaccessibility of the site to fire trucks, concrete was chosen as the building material. There were no ready-mix trucks available then, and the first floor of the house, incorporating the stairway as an integral part, was cast in a continuous forty-eight–hour pour, using a single cement mixer, under the direction of architect William Alexander.

Right

This gossamer tension stairway in a garden court at Rockefeller University in New York City was designed in 1956 by landscape architect Daniel Urban Kiley. He notes that "it was built off the site in component parts, then erected directly on the site using stainless steel cables and turn buckles. White Vermont marble was set in the steel frames. The marble treads are secured by the steel angle frame."

Bottom

The supple, airy sweep of this open-riser, open-balustrade staircase at the Gemological Institute in Los Angeles was designed in 1957 by Richard Neutra.

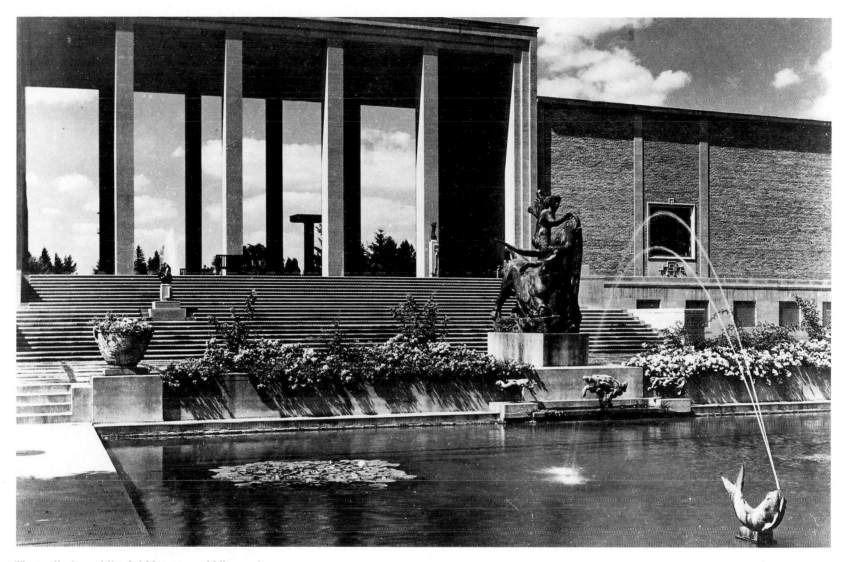

The south steps of the Art Museum and Library of
Cranbrook Academy of Art in Bloomfield Hills,
Michigan, lead from the Triton Pools to the entrance
under the lofty peristyle. Cranbrook's original
buildings were designed by Finnish architect, Eliel
Saarinen, who was the first president of the academy. The steps have been the set for films by
Charles Eames and the stage for fashion photogra-
phy and dance classes, as well as the site of gatherings,
reading, lounging, and studying since the early 1940s.

◁   Two noble lions guard the broad stairs that lead to
the Central Research Library of the New York
Public Library, where scholars and researchers from
the world over consult more than six million books
in over three thousand languages.

# 7 Garden Stairs

Chinese and Japanese, Islamic, classical French and Italian, scenic English: divergent philosophies of garden design meet in the cultivation of enclosed ground, the beautification of land for pleasure and delight. Most religions speak of a garden at the beginning of time and promise a garden at the end of life.

The world's topography has mountains, hills, and rolling land, prairies of grassland and meadows of flowers, jungles and deserts, oceans and lakes, streams and waterfalls. The garden offers control of these features. A roll of the land, a shrub-clad rise, a change of level, a lawn of grass, the colors of the season's flowers, a peaceful place to walk and sit, the fresh lushness of growing plants, and a pond or pool with the sound of splashing water—all these elements echo nature. In this miniaturization of nature's creations, this symbolic imitation of its features, shelters and paths, steps and stairs are constructed to provide access to the joys of the garden.

Many gardens extend over an area of different levels, sometimes steep enough to require steps or stairways. Garden steps range from simple stones set into a bank, to a grand sweep of stairs, dramatic, ornamented, and balustraded. They may be a few risers or a spill of steps that cascade from terrace to terrace, perhaps with bull-nosing of carved marble. They provide a geometric axis linking the topography and reflect the architecture of the time and place in which they were created.

A garden site with topographical variety is a challenging site. Villa Lante, one of the great gardens of Italy, clings to a hillside above the colorful little town of Bagnaia. Narrow cobbled streets lead to the gates of the villa, which was begun in 1566 for the bishop of Viterbo. A network of ornate steps and stairways ascend from the plateau of the formal garden to the twin villas, splitting, reuniting and curving around stepped cascades with flowing water banisters that spill into a pool at the base. The steps continue to rise in geometrical progression beside fountains and around them to the top of the hill, where the cultivated garden gives way to the wild. There at the head of the stairs is the water source, a natural spring channeled through the mouth of a stone mask set high on a bank of dripping moss.

East of Rome is the garden of Villa d'Este at Tivoli. In 1550 Cardinal Ippolito II d'Este took his appointment as governor of Tivoli, a consolation for not attaining the papacy. There he transformed a decrepit convent into a princely palace, aided by the Mannerist architect Pirro Ligorio, who designed the vast, magnificent garden as an architectural composition. While its form is not as classic and highly regarded as Villa Lante, it is spectacular and the more popular with its whimsies, frivolities, and conceits of fantastic fountains, sculpture, and cascades linked by a network of stairways.

Ninety years after the gardens at Villa Lante were planned, the most influential landscape designer of the time, André Le Nôtre (1613–1700), began his first commission for Nicolas Fouquet, the finance minister under young Louis XIV of France. At the château of Vaux-le-Vicomte, Le Nôtre enlarged the traditions of formal gardens and defined the French garden. When the minister, who outshone his monarch with his opulent residence, was imprisoned in 1664 for mismanagement of

Garden steps with foliaged risers, Mexico City.

One of the opulently balustraded garden staircases at Haddon Hall, Derbyshire, England. Construction of the semifortified manor house began in Norman times.

Opposite
Villa Torlonia in Frascati, Italy, was designed in 1623 by Carlo Maderna. In its garden an eight-tiered cascade of water is embraced by two great flights of bull-nosed, pitted travertine stairs that follow the curves of the basins, uninterrupted by landings.

the treasury, Louis XIV engaged his garden designer par excellence, and the lengthy and costly work on the hunting lodge of Versailles began. At Versailles, Le Nôtre still controls and choreographs the visitors by the placement of stairs, which lead from one view terrace to another by wide central stairways, narrow side stairways, long ramps, and to the Orangery by two ponderous flights of one hundred steps each. Versailles has been universally adopted as the model for palatial gardens: grand garden stairs and terraces throughout the world have been built on axial vista lines in imitation.

A wave of romanticism inspired eighteenth-century landscape designers to replace the old formal gardens in England with carefully planned natural landscaping, hiding any space-enclosing fences in ditches and de-emphasizing the importance of necessary steps and stairs, integrating them with the look of untouched nature. Although this new style was popular, it was also controversial, viewed as destructive of the old formality, soft, smooth, or too much like a landscape painting.

Islamic gardens, which originated where water was scarce, symbolized paradise. Because of that scarcity, waterways and pools were shallow, often lined with blue tiles to create the illusion of greater depth. Following the Arab conquest, which began in the seventh century along the Mediterranean, features of the Islamic garden design began to appear in Europe. The Islamic garden enclosures, walled against the climate, influenced the courtyard garden of Spain, with the extensive use of tiles laid in bright, geometric patterns on walls, fountains, and stairways. Patterned tile steps at the Alhambra and the Generalife Palace, both begun in 1350, show their Islamic heritage and still influence gardens as far away as Mexico and California.

The Chinese took pleasure in the spiritual calm of the landscape and its elements—sky, sea, mountain, and rock—which they considered fellow inhabitants with man in a crowded world. Their gardens represented nature's scenery, avoiding symmetry as nature does. Chinese stairways were usually of two types: formal, stylized stairs leading to shrines or pavilions; haphazard stair formations of natural rocks climbing steep garden paths. Destructive forces during the twentieth century have damaged many old Chinese gardens, but paintings showing the original form remain and some of them have been restored.

Garden design in Japan derived from the model of Chinese gardens. But by the year 1000 the Japanese had developed their own stylized form: traditional elements of the Chinese garden had been symbolized and scaled to the area to be landscaped. A mound could be a mountain and a pond an inlet of the ocean, to reproduce the spirit not the features of the natural landscape. Intricate rules and classifications govern the design of Japanese gardens. The stairs may be broad and bold, hewn of stone blocks, or simply natural rocks seemingly placed at random. In the beautiful gardens of Kyoto, the hilly terrain offers a perfect setting for every variety of steps and stairways—some with rock risers and treads of compacted earth, broad enough for several strides on each of them; some with narrow and precipitous steps, blocks of sculpture climbing a steep hill to a shrine.

The American garden is heir to all the world's influences. In 1851 the New York legislature passed the first Park Act, a milestone in the provision of land for the enjoyment of the public. When the land for Central Park was acquired, Frederick Law Olmsted (1822–1903) was appointed its superintendent. Olmsted had visited the Bois de Boulogne, the 1,100 acres (445 ha) of woods on the outskirts of Paris, and Birkenhead Park in a new suburb of

The first stairway inside the park surrounding the Villa Lante in Bagnaia, Italy, curves around a semicircular wall that encloses a fountain, which shoots a rainbow-catching, fine-misted jet of water two stories into the air, up to the level of the balustrade on the stairs that rise above it and lead to the parterre area of the formal gardens.

TOP RIGHT
This unusual double staircase in the Parque Güell in Barcelona was designed by Antoni Gaudí (1852–1926), the unconventional architect of Spain.

Liverpool, which had originated the country park when it opened in 1847. He was impressed by both its public ownership and its layout of lakes and paths. By 1858 2,500 men were at work landscaping Central Park, and water was let into the lake so that public skating could begin. Among the many and varied steps in this well-loved park is the monumental double staircase with two great flights of stairs on each side spilling down to the Esplanade.

The United States developed its own style of gardens often devoted to a single species of plant, such as the Magnolia Garden near Charleston, South Carolina, and the azalea garden at the Callaway Garden, south of Atlanta, Georgia, where the late industrialist Carson Callaway in 1950 began to create a garden that he vowed would be "the greatest since Adam was a boy!" The Huntington Botanical Garden in San Marino, California, offers eighteen different garden areas, including

a desert section with the largest collection of cacti in the world, a Japanese garden, a Shakespeare garden, and a lush rose garden. At Ohme Garden, a uniquely American garden that covers a boulder-strewn bluff above the Columbia River and the Wenatchee Valley in central Washington, steps and stairways of flat stones meander among the natural rock formations.

More modest gardens throughout the country—fenced, designed with steps and stairs, tended and privately owned—are a source of American pride. Contemporary American gardens are often extended living areas beyond the interior confines of the buildings. The accessible, livable, surfaced area with a direct relationship to the building has added the borrowed word *patio* to the American vocabulary. Outdoor living areas have become more complex and cultivated, with changing levels and steps and stairways to reach them.

This idyllic garden stairway of natural stones lined with bright ferns connects fourteenth-century Scotney Castle at Laberhurst, Kent, with a nineteenth-century manor house on top of the hill.

TOP LEFT
At Villa Lante the Water Chain, a long sloping cascade gushing from the mouth of a stone crayfish, is flanked by hedges and stone steps that accompany it until it floods the Fountains of the Giants below.

At Villa d'Este, shallow risers and deep ramped treads allow an easy ascent on steps beside water bubbling from a series of small basins, which give the stairs the name *Cordonato dei Bollori*, or Boiling Water Steps. As the hillside grows steeper, the shallow steps are transformed into a stairway with treads and risers of normal proportions. Throughout the garden, steps and stairs score the slopes, climbing among thunderous water displays in as much variety as the fountains themselves.

Its sandstone walls and balustrades richly ornamented, the grand double staircase in Central Park, New York, descends to the esplanade at Bethesda Fountain. Carvings on the extended balustrades on each landing represent the four seasons. This photograph is half of a stereograph taken about 1890, when the park was young.

TOP RIGHT
Stone lions, heads turned to the stairs, top the balustrades of these monumental stone stairways flanking a fountain grotto at Vaux-le-Vicomte, André Le Nôtre's first great garden commission.

RIGHT
On a steep site in the Santa Monica Mountains, landscape architects Galper/Baldon Associates held back the hill with terraces, the first of which contains the swimming pool behind a sloped wall of pebbled concrete. Four pebbled steps give access to the shallow water of the L-shaped pool. Further steps lead to a diving platform and from there to a terrace elevated to catch the last of the afternoon sun. The hill behind the pool is a tropical jungle of palms and tree ferns.

OPPOSITE
The mansion of Dumbarton Oaks in the Georgetown section of Washington, D.C., was owned by Robert Woods Bliss when the gardens were developed (1921–47) under the guidance of landscape architect Beatrix Ferrand. The horseshoe stairway, which circles a fountain, leads to the swimming pool.

OPPOSITE
TOP LEFT
The hundreds of gardens on the grounds of shrines
and temples in Kyoto are threaded with stairs of
every imaginable design. Here a gentle slope is
ascended by low risers of natural rock and very
deep treads.

TOP RIGHT
Soft treads of moss balustraded by foam flower lead
down from dining terrace to lawn in this Worcester,
Massachusetts, garden designed by Fletcher Steele
in 1940.

BOTTOM LEFT
Many public gardens in America incorporate
Japanese designs, authentic in concept and detail-
ing. Here steps form the arch of a bridge in the
Bellingrath Garden near Mobile, Alabama.

BOTTOM RIGHT
In the Japanese Tea Garden in Golden Gate Park,
San Francisco, cleatlike treads facilitate the steep
climb over a high arched bridge.

A classic Italian stairway of seventy steps bordered
by shaped yews descends through seven terraces
to the edge of Lake Waban. The garden of the
country estate at Wellesley, Massachusetts, was
begun in 1844 by Horatio Hollis Hunnewell, whose
aim was to collect every conifer that could survive
the New England winters. The estate is still owned
by the Hunnewell family.

# 8
# Steps to Water

Second only to the air we breathe, water—the ancestral cradle common to all—is of vital importance to us, but unlike air, water must be found and stored. Much time and effort has been spent in trying to find water, reach it, store it, and on occasion to tame or flee it, for all too often water is either insufficient or abundant to the point of being life-threatening. In some areas of the world, water is more important than life itself, for water *is* life.

Steps and stairways are often the means of reaching water—steps to rivers and streams; to cisterns and wells; and to lakes and pools. To contain and tame water, dams and dykes, reservoirs and water towers have been built, usually reached by means of steps and stairs. The first steps to water occurred along riverbeds with steep banks, making the water difficult to reach. Protruding rocks or roots and brush served as footholds and handholds on the path to the water and were augmented with step holes dug into the dirt, rocks, and logs, creating stairways to favorite places for drinking and bathing, to flat stones for washing clothes, and to fords and ferries.

Some remnants of ancient steps to water still exist, including the stairway down to the Persian well in Mycenae, a prehistoric Greek fortress city. This site, occupied since the early Bronze Age, is one of the most ancient cities in Greece and home of the legendary King Agamemnon. Just beyond the city wall near a small gateway in the northeastern section of the citadel is the Persian well, an underground cistern fed by the Persian spring that supplied the citadel with water. A broad stairway of irregular flat rocks leads to the water basin 38 feet

(11.5 m) below ground level.

To the ancient fortified hill cities of Israel, often under siege, water supply accessible to the citizens and not to their enemies was life itself. The water system in Megiddo, Israel, is fed by a spring deep underground, reached by a stairway hewn into the rock. The ancient fortress town of Megiddo, which overlooks the Plain of Esdralon (today the Valley of Jesreel) was first built about 3500 B.C. on a hilltop site that had been occupied by man from about 8000 B.C. The site has a bloody history as a battlefield—the name, Armageddon, means Hill of Megiddo—because it was situated at a strategic intersection of two important trade and military routes. In the beginning of the

OPPOSITE
**Well-worn steps lead to the Nile and a place to launder clothing.**

◁ **Steps to the swimming pool or public bath at Masada, located south of Jerusalem on the banks of the Dead Sea in Israel. Masada is renowned as a bastion of Jewish resistance because less than one thousand of its citizens defended it with their lives against the vastly superior might of the Romans, who finally prevailed but could not subjugate the Masada zealots, who committed suicide to avoid capture. The public swimming pool or ritual bath with plastered stairs leading down into the water was discovered when Masada was excavated in 1963–65. In the stone walls surrounding the pool were niches where the bathers could store their clothing while they used the pool.**

121

The engineers of King Ahab (874–853 B.C.) built the shaft and stairway down to the water table at Hazor in Israel. The stairs are wide enough to have accommodated pack animals or jar-laden women going up or coming down at the same time. The bottom four treads, in contact with the water, are basalt slabs.

TOP RIGHT

The steep stairway in the shaft dug in 1200 B.C. from the town of Megiddo, built on a rocky hilltop, to the spring at the base of the hill, which served as the town's water supply. When the shaft had reached its desired depth, one crew dug horizontally toward the spring while another dug from the spring toward the shaft and the stairs. When they met after digging a tunnel 169 feet (51.5 m) long, high enough for women to walk through carrying water jars, an error of less than two feet (61 cm) had been made. Nothing in archaeological history reveals a more sophisticated technique for so early a date. With its water supply secured, the city became impregnable.

town's history, its all-important water supply could be reached only by leaving the protection of the city walls, walking down the steep hill, and entering a deep cavern to an underground spring. To safeguard the women and children who fetched the water and in an effort to make the city safe from siege, ancient engineers in about 1200 B.C. sank a wide, stepped shaft from the city atop the hill down through the rubble of early settlements to the soft limestone where the spring was accessible.

The system at Hazor cuts down to the water table, and being within the city walls, was invulnerable. Now a dirt-covered ruin west of Jerusalem, Hazor was an ancient hill city, already important when it was expanded and well fortified

by King Solomon in the tenth century B.C. It was to become the city of King Ahab (874–853 B.C.), builder of the water system. Archaeologists found a large rectangular shaft, dug through the earth and retained by stone walls, that continued into the rock. The shaft contained five flights of wide stairs that led to the natural water table under the city and not to a spring outside the wall, as expected.

The water system built in 36–30 B.C. by King Herod at the fortress of Masada on top of an inaccessible hill, where there were no springs and it was impossible to reach any water table, consisted of huge cisterns with a capacity close to 1.5 million cubic feet (40,000 m³) scooped out of the rock. There are tall, narrow single flights of plastered stairs to the bottom of the

The steps that lead down to the banks of the Ganges River in India, like this one in the city of Varanasi, are called *ghat*, which in Hindu means stairway. The 350 million Hindus hold the Ganges sacred, continuing a long tradition. In cities and hamlets along the river's meandering 1,500 miles (2,414 km) from the Himalayas to the Bay of Bengal, *ghats* lead down to the sacred waters, where pious Hindus wash away their sins.

BOTTOM LEFT

In Tai O, on the island of Lantau in Hong Kong's harbor, broad steps lead to a shaded ferry boat crossing the canal that divides the village.

These steps to the Pasig River, just south of Manila in the Philippines, were used to wash laundry when this stereograph was taken in 1899.

STEPS TO WATER  123

Stone steps rise to a platform that surrounds the once vital and socially important wellhead in the city of San Gimignano, Italy.

Top Right
Broad steps descend from a colonnaded portico into the Roman bath in the town of Bath on the Avon River in England, founded by the Romans as Aquae Solis and dedicated to the deity Sul of Minerva. The Romans lined the bath with lead from nearby Mendip Hills, and today hot mineral water still gushes through lead-lined conduits into the bath-swimming pool. The town of Bath has developed into an elegant and popular British resort.

cistern cavities, which were fed by dams and aqueducts routing rainwater to the holding pools.

The Masada bathing pool is the earliest such facility yet found in Israel but earlier public baths have been found in Pompeii, Sabian (120 B.C.), and Forum (80 B.C.), and they were probably influenced by the earlier Greek gymnasia. The heated baths, or *thermae*, and the huge unheated pool, or *frigidarium*, were entered by marble steps that often stretched the entire length of the pool. Underwater steps in modern swimming pools require highly resistant materials and sturdy construction, and their risers may be higher than the standard riser since buoyancy increases as a person descends the steps into the water.

Steps down to water along rivers and canals range from the humble bamboo ladders of the families on the klong water-ways of Bangkok, to the many splendid steps to the waters in Venice, where every palace and hotel, every street and plaza, has steps and stairs that give people access to the gondolas and motor launches that ply the canals. In cities that are closely identified with a river—from Paris and the Seine, London and the Thames, Vienna and the Danube, to Cairo and the Nile, Nanking and the Yangtze, Varanasi and the Ganges, and Saint Louis, Memphis, New Orleans and the Mississippi— the steps and stairways that provide access to the water are as important as the bridges that cross it and the quays that line it.

TOP
Venetians and tourists alike can take a long lunch in the outdoor cafe at the top of the high bank of steps that leads to the canal where it flows under the arched Rialto bridge.

BOTTOM
The stairs to this fountain in Assisi, Italy, show the wear of generations of women who, before their houses had indoor plumbing, came here to fetch water and socialize.

◁ Gondoliers in Venice tend their crafts and chat, lounging on steps that lead from the walkway to the gondolas and waterways.

In the five-century-old city of Barcelona, the Parc de l'Espagna Industrial, designed by architect Luis Peña-Ganchequi, with its stadiumlike embankment of steps down to the water, is as new as the suburbs that surround it.

BOTTOM LEFT
Broad underwater steps permit successively deeper wading in this swimming pool, built on the site of an abandoned distillery in Cuernavaca, Mexico. The roof was removed, but the supporting pillars were retained.

BOTTOM RIGHT
The Tiber River, which flows through Rome between high embankments, can be reached by a combination of stairways that allow pedestrians access to the walkways along the water.

Tiled in the glow of toy red that promises the heat of the water, this spa in a large condominium complex in Los Angeles offers two entrances to its therapeutic bubbles. The handrail backed by a rounded groove in the wall emphasizes the access. Designed by Galper/Baldon Associates of Venice, California.

Rock steps lead to the women's bathing pool at Takaragawa Onsen, a natural mineral hot springs in Gumma Prefecture, Japan.

Where a sloped site dictated that the pool be below the patio level, a bank of rock stairs descends to the water and surrounding deck in a garden in Los Angeles.

Broad steps lead down on all sides into this ▷ swimming pool in Palm Springs, California. The building, designed in the 1950s by architects Clark and Frey, shows an early experiment with solar heating control. The funnel extensions of different lengths over the circular windows regulate the direct sunshine entering the building.

OPPOSITE
Staircase leading to the magnificent Neptune swimming pool at Hearst Castle in San Simeon, California, one of the most fantastic private residences in the world. The publisher William Randolph Hearst constructed the main residence, La Casa Grande, and three guest houses on the estate from 1919 to 1947 and left it to the State of California when he died in 1951. San Simeon and the marble Neptune pool, which is 104 feet (31.7 m) long, were designed by the architect Julia Morgan.

# 9
# Interior Staircases

Interior stairways are often located close to the entry, immediately seen, a usable sculpture beckoning the climb. Particularly in public buildings, the design of such stairways is frequently opulent and grand, an indulgence of rich materials. Protected from the wear of weather, the interior stairway can be carpeted or painted, mirrored or gilded, polished and waxed, and lit with crystal chandeliers. It may be a feat of engineering; or it may be ornate and imposing, at times more interesting than the building itself, a spectacular, theatrical setting to impress the patrons.

Most staircases in public buildings, however, are utilitarian, bland, and uninspired. In modern high rises with their speedy elevators, they are usually simply auxiliary or for use in an emergency. Even an ordinary staircase may have a moment of glory. for instance, when such a building is in the framing stage and presents only a gridwork of iron, the multiple flight of stairway structures already welded into place form an intricate pattern, soon to disappear forever, walled into the finished building. Such a pattern of stairways is, however, revealed behind a towering glass wall for the entire height of the Hong Kong and Shanghai Bank in Hong Kong.

Many of the great stairways of the world are enhanced by their settings; colonnaded arcades, domed rotundas, skylit atriums, or marble stairwells. Under painted ceilings of heavenly scenes, a number of great baroque stair halls, larger than many houses, are entirely devoted to the celebration of the spacious banks of grand staircases. The German stair hall is called a *Treppenhaus*, literally stair house, and one of the grandest examples is found at Würzburg. Grand stairs, also called imperial stairs, include such impressive examples as the Scala Regia in the Vatican palace, designed 1663–66, by Giovanni Lorenzo Bernini who progressively shortened the columns that line the stairs on either side, creating an exaggerated perspective.

A stairway that leads down usually is associated with less attractive destinations, such as furnace cellars or mausoleum crypts, while traditionally stairways leading up are associated with desirable, hallowed, and lofty destinations, such as royal thrones, pulpits, or a good seat at the baseball stadium. At the Smithsonian Institution in Washington, D.C., architect Jean Paul Carlhian had to provide an interesting access down to a three-story underground museum, housing centers for African, Near Eastern, and Asian cultures, constructed under a garden. To counteract a potentially negative mood, Carlhian provided access through two attractive garden pavilions, each housing a monumental staircase below a series of bright skylights. The attractive design dispels any adverse connotation of descent. The staircase in the pavilion at the African center has a circular pattern around the skylit shaft, while the Near Eastern and Asian centers are reached by a staircase that separates diagonally into two as it descends and reunites around the shaft, coaxing a downward movement.

A stairway in a private residence is more personal than a stairway anywhere else. Everyone has a childhood memory of a stairway, perhaps in a grandmother's house or a childhood home. It may have been the link from the living space below to the more private world above, where

The grand staircase in the Painted Hall at Chatsworth in Derbyshire, England. Originally a twin-armed curved staircase designed by the First Duke of Devonshire, William (1640–1707), occupied the space. The Sixth Duke, William Spencer (1780–1858), and his architect, Wyatville, replaced it with a single staircase so steep that it was uncomfortable. This staircase was in turn replaced by the Ninth Duke, Victor Christian William (1868–1938), who in 1912 built a more massive, less steep staircase, improving it by increasing the number of steps and adding a landing after the first twelve steps, which made the structure extend farther into the hall. That is the staircase that stands in the Painted Hall today.

The justly famous Queen's Staircase at Versailles was created by Louis Le Vau (1612–70) for Queen Marie-Thérèse d'Autriche. The massive balustrade with close-set, red marble balusters is topped by a banister of black marble.

OPPOSITE
The grand staircase of the Bourbon Royal Palace at Caserta was built by the future Charles III of Spain after he conquered Naples in 1734 and designed by architect Luigi Vanvitelli (1700–73) of Naples. Two magnificent stone lions guard the landing of this immense baroque stair hall.

the child was at first confined. Initially
carried up and down those stairs, eventu-
ally the child learned to maneuver them
without assistance, climbing down back-
wards, at first on hands and knees in
intimate contact with treads and risers,
probably falling down them more than
once. At times the boy may have sneaked
down those stairs, when he should have
been upstairs in bed; and he would have
seen his mother on the stairs, unfamiliar in
her party finery, ready to go out and
leave him with a stranger. Later his sister
stood there, too, in her first high heels,
smiling at a frightened neighbor boy
waiting in awe in the hall below. The
father, at festivities in his own home,
would bound halfway up the stairs to get
above the heads of the guests to toast a
new year or announce a family event,
while the children huddled on the landing
above, peering through the banister. And
there may have been cellar stairs as well,
stairs of mystery, dim and steep, and
sometimes featured in bad dreams. Or an
attic stair, also steep, hardly more than a
ladder folding down out of a hole in the
ceiling and leading to the past, where
pieces of yesteryear were stored among
the cobwebs.

A stairway may evoke a vision of its
former owner. Climbing the ordinary,
dingy, and slightly dank stairway to the
corner apartment at 2 Sadovaya-Kudrin-
skaya Ulitza in Leningrad, where Dostoy-
evski wrote *The Brothers Karamazov* in
1880, you can almost hear the tubercular
cough that took this great writer the
following year on a cold February day. On
a sidestreet in Copenhagen are the first
lodgings of Hans Christian Andersen,
beloved Danish fairy tale writer, which he
took in 1819 when, barely fifteen years
old, he came to the city from his native
Odense to seek fame and fortune. At the
house where he found a tiny upstairs,
windowless room—a larder, in fact—off
the kitchen of his widow landlady, in the

Michelangelo's sketch for the hidden stairway between the shells of the double dome he designed for Saint Peter's in the Vatican City, the world's largest Christian church.

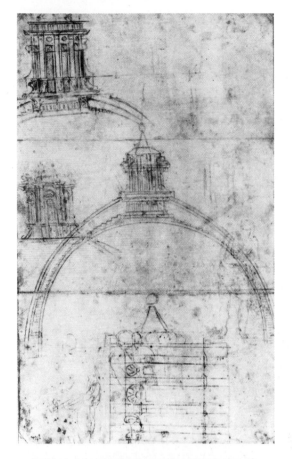

city's red light district, young Hans Christian would bound up a simple flight of stairs to his own little world, to dream stories that one day would delight all readers.

The unusual, oval-shaped spiral staircase, designed by the English architect Robert Adam in 1777, was commissioned by David Kennedy, the Tenth Earl of Cassilis, for his ancestral home, Culzean Castle in Scotland. The stairway is ingeniously planned so that at each landing the climber is given a choice of turning either right or left.

Among the more impressive private residences in the United States, architecturally if not historically, are those built during the Gilded Age in Newport, Rhode Island. On Bellevue Avenue, for example, stands The Elms, the Edwin Berwind House, a mansion designed by Horace Trumbauer and built in 1901–02. Inside, a magnificent double staircase rises from the foyer. On the same street is Rosecliff, the J. Edgar Monroe House, which was modeled after the Grand Trianon at Versailles and designed by Stanford White of

The hidden stairway between the two shells of the double dome designed by Filippo Brunelleschi (1377–1446) for the duomo in Florence can still be climbed, bringing tourists to a panoramic view of the city roofs.

BOTTOM RIGHT
Stairway between the two shells of the golden dome of the Iowa State Capitol. Begun in 1871 and completed in 1886, this was Iowa's sixth capitol building and the second to be located in Des Moines.

OPPOSITE
The grand staircase on the French transatlantic ocean liner SS *Paris* was photographed in 1921. Launched in 1916, it was the flagship of the French Line. The great liners of the twentieth century were floating palaces of stunning opulence, their staircases rivaling the most ornate and elaborate ones ashore.

In Hardwick Hall, Derbyshire, the most beautiful and least altered of Elizabethan manor houses in England, each course of a state dinner had to travel in ceremonial procession from the kitchens below up the stone flights of stairs to the high great chamber where the banquet took place.

TOP RIGHT
Marble staircase in the Library of Congress, Washington, D.C., designed by the architectural firm Smithmeyer and Pelz and completed in 1897.

OPPOSITE
The imposing staircase at the Palace of Justice in Vienna, completed in 1881, is topped by a ten-foot (3 m) marble statue of Justice.

McKim, Mead & White. Its elegant stairway is framed by a heart-shaped aperture accented with the elaborate tracery of its iron balustrade.

In the magnificent sixteenth-century manor house of Chatsworth in Derbyshire, England, a grand staircase with gilded balustrades graces the south end of the Painted Hall. Chatsworth was built by Sir William Cavendish and his wife Elizabeth Hardwick in the mid-1550s. Sir William died in 1557, and forty years later, Elizabeth, at seventy years of age upon the death of her fourth husband, began the construction of yet another manor house, Hardwick Hall in Derbyshire. Hardwick Hall has a staircase like no other. Excep-

tionally broad with low risers and made of stone, it wanders through the house like a street passage, from landing to landing. The upper flights are made of wood and are as bare of any decoration as the stone stairs below. In places the stairs curve around a newel to become a spiral, when space for it is constricted. There are no handrails, no carpeting, no embellishments. It is an extraordinary concept. Little that is the work of Bess of Hardwick remains unremodeled at Chatsworth, but Hardwick Hall is much as she left it. She knew the importance of making stairways an attractive part of a house: unlike furnishings, they remain when the first occupants move on.

A fine small staircase with a combination of curved and straight flights of marble steps rises three stories through a narrow, skylit shaft, cutting its way through the curio-cabinet house of John Soane at No. 13 Lincoln's Inn Fields in London. By 1830, Soane had become the dean of the British architectural establishment. An avid collector of paintings and sculptures, architectural fragments and memorabilia, and various artistic bric-a-brac, Soane carefully designed his neoclassic house, now a museum, to accommodate these possessions.

The staircase at Herstmonceux Castle, East Sussex, England, is a structure that results more from the cabinetmaker's art than that of the carpenter. Wooden stairways such as this one, with its encasements and panels, wood balustrades, and newels crowned with elaborate finials, were the contribution of Tudor England to Renaissance architecture.

The huge interior glass-covered court of the Bradbury Building in Los Angeles is a giant sculpture of balconies reached by caged elevators and flights of ornate, cast-iron stairways. Designed by George H. Wyman and built in 1893, the building, named for its owner, was a unique structure in the still-formative city.

The segregated stairways in the entry hall of the Center Family Dwelling House in Shaker Village. The religious sect was founded in 1776 and so called, derisively, because of the custom of dancing in a frenzy of religious ecstasy. Stairways at the restored Shaker Village of Pleasant Hill, Kentucky were designed to accommodate the celibate inhabitants. Separate entrances and dual staircases, one for the brethren and one for the sisters, led to their separate apartments.

OPPOSITE
TOP LEFT

Stairways usually lead somewhere, but this stairway in the whimsical, 160-room Winchester House in San Jose, California, dead-ends at the ceiling. In another room of the house, two facing stairways both lead only to the ceiling. Mrs. Winchester, who was obsessed with the occult, hoped that the evil ghosts visiting her home would bump their heads on the ceiling if they tried to mount the aimless stairs.

BOTTOM LEFT

Staircases in seventeenth-century New England houses were apt to be steep and narrow. This staircase leads to the upstairs bedrooms in the Parson Capen House in Topsfield, Massachusetts, which was built in 1683.

RIGHT

The staircase in the grand hall of Victorian Iolani Palace in Honolulu. Built by King David Kalahaua and completed in 1882, the palace is the only state residence of royalty in the United States. Used by the kings of Hawaii as their official residence, the one hundred-room, brick and stucco mansion also served as the capitol for the Republic of Hawaii, the Territory of Hawaii, and finally of the new state government until a new state capitol was completed in 1969. When architectural restoration of the Iolani Palace was completed in 1977, the rich wooden staircase with its sculptured finials had regained its former splendor.

The repetition of stairways rising from floor to floor creates abstract patterns: in the Town Hall of Lyngby-Taarbaek, Denmark, ca. 1954; at Rockfeller University Hospital in New York; and in an aging anonymous house nearing demolition.

The *hako-kaidan*, which translates from the Japanese as box stairway, uses the spaces underneath the treads and risers for cupboards and drawers. This box staircase in Imari, Kyushu, is a beautiful example of the fine woodwork of the best Japanese master cabinetmakers.

Beyond the arched colonnade of the Imperial Hotel in Vienna is a perfect miniature grand stairway. On its closed string runs an elaborate iron balustrade, brass railed, with an intricate iron newel. Its marble steps, culminating in curtail treads, have a carpet runner held by brass rods.

In the Louvre, Paris, a dimly lit flight of stone steps leads to a landing where the marble statue of Nike, the Goddess of Victory, also known as Winged Victory of Samothrace, stands bathed in a burst of natural daylight. Headless, armless, breasts thrust forward and garments flowing about her, she was found in 1863 on Samothrace, a Greek island in the Aegean, probably erected there by Rhodians about 203 B.C. to commemorate a sea battle.

In 1898 the Belgian architect Victor Horta built a beautiful house for himself on rue Americaine in Brussels. He designed the splendid staircase of this house with attenuated, flowing, naturalistic lines characteristic of the Art Nouveau style. Though there had been portents of this distinctive style, the four-story Hotel Tassel with its octagonal stair hall, designed by Horta in 1892, is deemed to have begun the Art Nouveau movement.

When the renowned Spanish architect Antoni Gaudí in 1905–07 remodeled Casa Batlló in Barcelona, he spun a curve of soft-sculptured, brown wood stairway set in a white plaster hall, achieving a pleasing, ornamental effect. The house itself is called "The House of Bones," because of the bonelike columns framing the windows.

Perhaps the best-known staircase in a Paris business establishment is the mirrored one in the salon established by Gabrielle "Coco" Chanel in 1921 at 31, rue Cambon. The faceted mirrors of its beautiful curved staircase create an illusion of infinite space and continue to reflect the beautiful models descending season after season to the salon below to show the Chanel lines. A replica of Chanel's stairway was seen by a wide audience in 1969, recreated on stage in the musical *Coco*, in which Katharine Hepburn portrayed the couturiere.

The main staircase of the town hall at Rødovre,    ▷
Denmark, was designed in 1956 by the Danish architect Arne Jacobsen. This attenuated structure with ratchet-shaped metal stringer and rods hangs self-contained in the stairwell.

Creating unprecedented, nontraditional forms in postrevolutionary Russia, architect Ilya Golosov coiled a blunt, simple staircase in a glassed corner tower of the Yuyev Workers Club, completed in Moscow in 1926.

The grand double staircase at The Elms in Newport, Rhode Island, outlines and encircles the entry foyer, with its top flight forming a sheltering canopy over the tall, arched front entry. The mansion is a close copy of Mansart's 1750 Château d'Agnès at Asnières near Paris, with some alterations of the façade.

At Rosecliff in Newport, Rhode Island, beyond the entry vestibule, and through a Palladian arch supported by columns, is the stair hall and an elegant curve of rococo stairs with an intricately fashioned wrought-iron balustrade. The steps, made of pale Caen limestone, end with six curtailed treads.

Two long hallways extend to north and south from the central rotunda of the handsome capitol building in Des Moines, Iowa. At the end of each hallway is a double staircase to the Senate or House chambers above. The staircases are made of iron, their balustrades and risers bronze finished. The treads are tile laid in patterns, and the hand rails are oak and walnut native to Iowa.

Architect Ricardo Legorreta was asked to design a staircase with low risers that looked easy to climb in an office building in Mexico City to lure tenants and visitors away from the elevator, which uses expensive electrical power. It worked.

At the Stuhr Museum at Grand Island, Nebraska, the complex, curved open stringers of the double staircase are echoed by the wooden handrails. The simple iron balusters, two to a tread, give an impression of lightness and grace to this design by architect Edward Durrell Stone.

The line of the dark banister traces the flight of stairs on the stark white wall of this Beverly Hills residence, designed by architect John Lautner. ▷

New York designer Joe D'Urso added a middle
third stringer to this starkly beautiful stairway,
turning the underside into sculpture.

This unusual stairway, designed by architect
Angelo Cortesis for a private home in Milan, is an
engineering feat: each tread and riser is a freestanding, up-ended, L-shaped structure, forming a
daring flight of stairs.

**This brilliant blue abstraction of stair forms is viewed from above at La Muralla Roja, designed by architect Ricardo Bofill.**

In his own home designed in the 1950s in Palm Springs, California, architect Albert Frey hung this stairway on stainless steel rods.

The dramatic use of changing levels and the steps connecting them creates a spectacular approach to the dining room of a residence in the mountains at Laurentides Park, Quebec.

Opposite
Like a flight of miniature bridges, wooden treads span a sloped surface that is gouged and painted to resemble a creek bed swollen with the water of the spring run-off. Water from a small fountain trickles down the gouges in the 1950 Cave Creek House by Paolo Soleri.

The architectural firm NBBJ Group remodeled a large turn-of-the-century warehouse in Seattle to serve as its headquarters. The exterior was virtually untouched, but inside a dramatic five-story, skylighted stairscape was created. Linking work areas as though they were separate buildings on a hillside, the staircases become the unifying element for the entire complex.

OPPOSITE
·At the Mission Inn in Riverside, California, a coil of stairs clings to the arcaded Rotunda Internacional, built to symbolize a desire for world peace, a 1929 addition to the inn that was begun in 1902.

The open prefabricated steel spiral stairway and open-grated decking allow light to filter to the floors below, creating an airy expanse of brightness, the goal of architect Carl Day.

This dramatic stairway provides a spectacular view of the lofty interior of the Banco de Londres in the financial district of Buenos Aires. It was designed in the late 1950s by architects Sanchez Elia, Clorindo Testa, and Peralta Ramos.

At the Museo Arte Contemporaneo Internacional ▷ Rufino Tamayo in Mexico City, a series of galleries on different levels, connected with steps in various configurations, overlooks a four-story central court with exhibits of sculpture. Designed in 1975, the architects were Abraham Zabludovsky and Gonzales de Leon.

# 10
# The Spiral Staircase

A staircase, circular in plan, with more or less wedge-shaped steps, their treads wider at one end than at the other, arranged to wind around a vertical pole, or newel, or surrounding a central open well, is commonly known as a spiral staircase. The popular spiral staircase is also called a circular or helical staircase; cockle or screw stair; a solid-newel or corkscrew stair, or caracol; and sometimes a cochlea, vice stair, or simply a winding staircase.

This form of staircase has been constructed and used for many centuries. During Roman times it had already developed into a well-understood, sophisticated form seen in the pillars of victory or memorial columns, the most famous of which is Trajan's Column, a Doric column over 100 feet (30 m) high with the entrance to the emperor's tomb in its pedestal. The shaft once contained a staircase that circled the central newel, the outer ends of its treads supported by the wall. To reach the top of the column of Marcus Aurelius, built in A.D. 174, one climbs 197 steps. In Thessalonika, the seat of the governor general of northern Greece, Saint George Church, believed to have been built over a Roman temple about 480 A.D., has one of the oldest still extant spiral staircases surrounding an open well. Thessalonika was founded in 315 B.C. by King Cassander of Macedonia who named the city after his wife, Thessalonika, the sister of Alexander the Great.

During the Romanesque period, the spiral staircase was increasingly used because it could be built into the solid masonry of the thick Romanesque walls and buttresses. The spiral stairs in the circular wells that flank the entry to the cathedral, built 796–804 by Emperor Charlemagne, at Aix-la-Chapelle are typical of this construction.

The treads of stone spiral staircases were often carved as one with a segment of the newel. The stacked segments became the cylinder around which the treads radiated, their outer ends embedded in the wall of the stairwell or stair tower. Because of the wedge-shaped form of the tread, a climber can accommodate a personal length of stride by placing the foot on the spot on the tread at whatever distance from the newel is most comfortable.

The spiral staircase is both space-saving and fits into awkward places, which has contributed to its lasting popularity. Much used in medieval architecture,

OPPOSITE
Painted to look like marble, the spiral staircase in the library of the Melk Monastery in Austria is a resplendent feature of this Benedictine monastery. Melk is a remarkable example of abbey architecture and a striking monument of the Baroque period. Built on the Danube between 1702 and 1714, it was designed by Jakob Prandtauer.

◁ The Leaning Tower of Pisa, begun in 1174 and finished in 1350 with an added belfry, is eight stories tall and now deviates about seventeen feet (5 m) from the perpendicular, a tilt that is felt clearly on the spiral staircase within.

The Scala del Bovolo, Palazzo Contarini in Venice, has a lacy, white marble staircase set in an elegant brick stair tower.

Top Right
**Common Wentletrap,** *Epitonium clathrus*.

spiral staircases are found in stàir towers and bell towers, including the *campaniles* of Italy, such as the Leaning Tower of Pisa. Stair towers evolved from solid masonry structures to creations of pillars and open arches. An exquisite example of such an open stair tower with a spiral staircase is the Scala del Bovolo, or Staircase of the Shell, so named because of its resemblance to a seashell. Located in the Palazzo Contarini in Venice and built during the latter part of the fifteenth century, its design is ascribed to Giovanni Candi.

Other spiral staircases have been named after seashells. At the Convent of San Domenico in the little town of Fiesole overlooking Florence, the exquisitely designed flight of eight steps leading down to the cloister is called the Scala della Conchiglia, after the conch shell.

The role of seashells as an inspiration in the design of spiral staircases is evident. Many prominent architectural writers have likened spiral staircases to the shells of sea creatures, notably Theodore Andrea Cook who pointed out that "architecture is full of copies from nature" and felt that

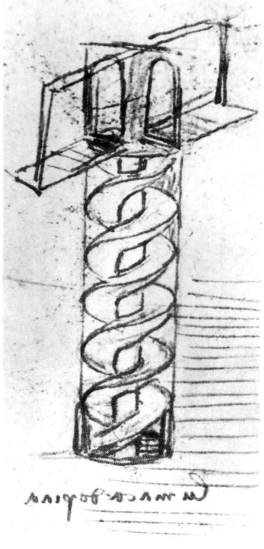

the architects of such staircases must have studied nature's spirals in the form of seashells.

The term *cockle stairs*, already in use in the seventeenth century, comes from cockle or cochlea, a shellfish with a spiral shell. *Cochlea*, to describe a spiral staircase, was in use even earlier. In 1538 the English antiquarian John Leland, in telling how in 1328 King Edward III wrested power from his mother, Isabella of France, and her lover and influential advisor, Roger Mortimer, by one night invading a council being held at Nottingham Castle and

taking Mortimer prisoner, wrote: "There is also a Chochlea with a turret over it where the Kepers of the Castelle say Edwarde the Thirdes Band came up through the Rok." Conversely, shells take their names from the latin word *scala*, meaning stair, such as the *scalaria scalaris*, *voluta scalaris*, *epitonium scalare*, and many more. One shell is commonly known as the Staircase Shell (*Architectonica troclearis*), a tropical shellfish that lives on sandy bottoms at moderate depths.

In the famous Renaissance château at Chambord (1519–47) in the Loire Valley

TOP LEFT
Measured drawing showing original staircase and apertures for illumination in the Column of Trajan.

CENTER
The primitive little church on the Acoma Indian Pueblo near Albuquerque, New Mexico, houses this simple spiral staircase. Steps and newel are cut from one piece of stone and stacked.

TOP RIGHT
Sketch for a double spiral staircase by Leonardo da Vinci.

The ornate, five-story spiral staircase in the law library of the state capitol building in Des Moines, Iowa. The building was completed in 1886, but most of the interior decoration was not undertaken until the turn of the century.

near Tours, there is a remarkable double spiral staircase. It contains two spirals, one within the other, so designed that one person may ascend and another descend without ever meeting or seeing one another, although their steps and voices can be heard plainly. The idea for a double spiral staircase did not originate with Domenico da Cortona, the architect who made many of the designs for Chambord; Leonardo da Vinci (1452–1519) made a sketch for one in the late fifteenth century.

The latter part of the Renaissance produced few innovations in the form and not many exciting examples of spiral staircases. But one outstanding example from this period is the spectacular spiral staircase in the Farnese villa at Caprarola, north of Rome. The five-sided palace and spiral staircase were designed by the Italian architect Giacomo da Vignola, who succeeded Michelangelo as chief architect of Saint Peter's in 1564. Frescoes in the stair tower depicting the civic contributions and achievements of the Farnese family were commissioned by Alessandro Farnese who, as Pope Paul III from 1534 to 1549, was a patron of the arts and architecture. Begun in 1547, the palace was not finished until 1559, a decade after the death of the patron pope.

To tend the beacon that guides ships at sea, lighthouse keepers climb to the top of a tower, usually on a spiral staircase. One such staircase made famous in folk ballads and seamen's lore can be found in the Eddystone Lighthouse, which stands in Plymouth Bay, England. The original lighthouse was built of timber in the 1690s, but in a great storm in 1703 it was demolished by the sea and swept away

with the man who designed it, Henry Winstanley. The replacement lighthouse, constructed of oak and iron, was destroyed by fire in 1775. The structure, including the interior spiral staircase, was rebuilt by John Smeaton entirely of interlocking stone, a revolutionary method of construction in those days. It stood until 1881, when it was replaced by the present Eddystone Lighthouse, which was designed by Sir James Douglas and stands 133 feet (40.5 m) above water, the top reached by a spiral staircase.

There was little technical development in the art of building spiral staircases until the nineteenth century when a variety of forms appeared, made possible by the discovery of new building materials and construction methods. In the mid-nineteenth century cast iron and wrought iron construction made possible such buildings as the famous Crystal Palace, built for the Great Exhibition in London in 1851, or the Great Palm House in Kew Gardens, the Royal Botanic Gardens outside London.

Later examples are the spiral staircases designed by the German architect and founder of the Bauhaus, Walter Gropius (1883–1967), for the Werkbund Exhibition in Cologne, Germany, in 1914, and the design by the Italian architect, Pier Luigi Nervi (1891–1969), for the city stadium in Florence.

The spiral staircase has had a modern renaissance because it is practical and esthetically pleasing where space is at a premium. Consequently a large variety of spiral stair components or prefabricated spiral staircases in many different materials and configurations are available today.

The low risers and deep, ramped treads of the ornate, double grand spiral staircase at the Vatican museums have provided comfortable ascent and descent for countless visitors.

Four hundred steps, a third of them on the outside of the spire of Our Saviour's Church in Copenhagen, lead to the gilt globe and Christ figure on top. The church was built between 1682 and 1696; the spire, acting as a newel for its distinctive spiral staircase designed by Lauridz de Thura, was completed in 1752.

Inside the Statue of Liberty, on Bedloe's Island in New York harbor, a spiral staircase winds its way to the top. The statue was designed by Frédéric-Auguste Bartholdi and presented to the United States by the Franco-American Union in 1884 to commemorate the French and American revolutions. Made of copper sheets, it stands 152 feet (43 m) tall on a massive granite face platform. It became a national monument in 1924 and was thoroughly renovated both inside and out in 1984.

OPPOSITE
The iron castings of the railing on this spiral staircase in the Palm House of Kew Gardens in London are palm motifs borrowed from Greek architecture. Designed by Burton and Turner, this impressive glass and iron greenhouse, built 1844–48 with the encouragement of Queen Victoria, contains two ornate spirals in the central gallery.

Spiral stairway to the beach at the Crane Beach Hotel on Barbados, an independent state in the West Indies and the most easterly of the Caribbean Islands.

Like a giant plaster spindle seashell augering itself into the sandy beach, this white staircase spiral gives access to a terrace overlooking the Pacific shore of Baja California in Mexico.

OPPOSITE
Made entirely of clear, transparent Lucite, this eye-catching staircase structure, which gathers and reflects the colors surrounding it, was made by Signatures in Acrivue.

This handsome prefabricated spiral staircase from the British manufacturer, Spiral Staircase Systems, has plexiglass treads resting on polished alloy brackets with an open stringer balustrade of tubular stainless steel, but any combination of aluminum, brass, or stainless steel can be used. Architects, Chapman Taylor Partnership.

Spiral staircase at the Shore Cliff Lodge & Inn at Pismo Beach, California, providing access to the beach from the palisades above.

The clean-lined metal spiral, corkscrewing up the wall of the gym hall at Stenhus Boarding School in Holbaek, Denmark, flings out a shadow alter ego like a dancing partner, to trace a free whirl on the wall.

The hanging spiral staircase in the lobby of the Water & Power Building in Los Angeles, was designed by architect A. C. Martin.

OPPOSITE
A sinuous stairway coils in one of the stair towers of the three-building complex known as Triennale di Milano.

Like another vine among the greenery, this spiral staircase by Duvinage climbs up its slender newel to the top floor of a remodeled Georgian town house in Washington, D.C.

Designer Paul Haig's spiral staircase enclosure in the form of a truncated Tuscan column, which stands in the New York showroom of Knoll Design Center, has an exaggerated base molding that continues on the rolling door. In the hollow interior of the column stands the bright turquoise steel stairs.

This sophisticated staircase tower is an unexpected presence in the backyard of a Copenhagen apartment building, soaring above the bicycle sheds like a gleaming silo.

The six-story spiral staircase in a government building in Vauxhall, London, was manufactured by Spiral Staircase Systems following a general layout by architects Chapman Taylor Partnership. The staircase stands beside twin exposed rocket-type elevators in the atrium and serves as additional access to all the floors. More than one hundred steel treads with rubber coverings and plaster soffits circle a steel central column. The balustrade is clear Lexan with a stainless-steel handrail.

This ten-story spiral staircase serves as a fire escape
for an apartment house in Zurich.

An unusual spiral staircase uses a brick chimney as
its central newel and recalls ancient configurations
that wind around carved stone newels. Architects,
Ford, Carson & Powell.

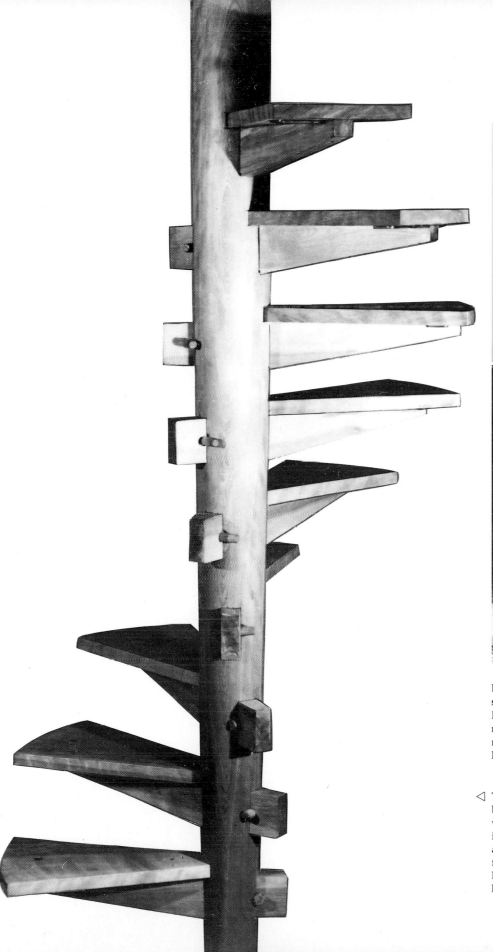

Like a graceful wood sculpture this prefabricated spiral staircase by Spiral Manufacturing of Baton Rouge, Louisiana, features an octagonal, curved newel of laminated wood, available in pine, oak, or maple. The pressure-laminated treads are rectangular in shape to provide better footing.

◁ This simple spiral staircase was handcarved in birch in the early 1940s and can be disassembled. It was not installed for the man who commissioned it, because he did not return from war. Its designer, architect William Alexander, bought back the stair from his client's family and kept it as a sculpture, leaning against a wall in his New York studio, until he installed it in his home in California.

A bright red solid spiral staircase dominates the large cube of space removed from the center of this twenty-story condominium building standing at the edge of Biscayne Bay, Florida. The patio created in the open space also holds a health club, a free-form spa, and palm trees. Winner of a Progressive Architecture Citation in 1980, The Atlantis was designed by Arquitectonica.

The summit of the spectacular spiral staircase at one of the "follies" in the Parc de la Villette in Paris, which is emerging as a most unusual public space. The huge futuristic complex, built on the former site of Paris's largest slaughterhouse, is a 136 acre (1.5 h) park that includes theaters, museums, and restaurants as well as an unusual sculpture garden. Thirty-four structures, all variations on a 36-foot (11 m) cube, are called follies by their creator, architect Bernard Tschumi and feature a variety of steps and stairways.

OPPOSITE

A precarious stair for an intrepid climber whirls to a loft. Designed by Pierre Botschi, the unusual spiral staircase stands in his mews house in London.

178  STEPS & STAIRWAYS

In creating this cast-aluminum spiral staircase for London's Science Museum, sculptor Michael Black was inspired by watching two swans copulating, their delicately tapered bodies close together, their long necks extended in apparent appreciation of the moment. He calls his work The Swan Staircase.

OPPOSITE
This massive yet elegant spiral stairway stands in the gleaming hallway of the home of its designer, Michael Kalil.

# 11
# Staircase Superstars

Staircases of all kinds have captured people's imagination, and everyone has a favorite staircase somewhere in the world. Some staircases of great stature and popularity have achieved international fame and have been the subjects of painters and photographers, writers and poets.

The criteria for singling out some staircases and affording them honorable mention as superstars are these: exceptional grandeur and beauty; historical significance; association with particularly charming or powerful legends; the most frequently mentioned as a favorite; impressive or landmark locations; scale; and finally the most frequently published. The breathtaking magnificence of the Grand Staircase of Würzburg Residence Palace and Napoleon's historic farewell address to his troops at the Horseshoe Staircase at Fontainebleau elevate those staircases to superstardom. The intriguing legend of the spiral stairway in the Loretto Chapel in Santa Fe, the enormous popularity of the Spanish Steps in Rome, and the spectacular location of the steep steps on the Great Wall of China are all perfect examples. These stairways, together with others, often publicized, have become singularly famous, indeed they are superstars.

Ricardo Bofill and the Taller de Arquitectura in 1974–76 created a monument at Le Perthus on the French/Spanish border to symbolize the identity of that region, Catalonia. History and nature inspired this spectacular stairway of heroic proportions, which rises to a monument on top of an earthen pyramid. With risers almost two feet (61 cm) high, the climb to the top is arduous. The clean lines of the man-made pyramid are a stylized evocation of the mountains of Catalonia.

The flag of Catalonia, four red stripes on a golden ground, derives from the medieval legend of Wilfredo el Velloso, who drew four bloody fingers across his golden shield before he died in battle and left the resulting design to comrades as their banner. The yellow structure on top of the pyramid suggests the golden shield, and four twisted and truncated pillars, the fingers. Down the sides of the grand stairway are interlocking discs of red brick symbolizing drops of blood.

From this magnificent staircase, which is both architecturally and historically important, Emperor Napoleon Bonaparte said farewell to his troops on April 20, 1814, after abdicating at the age of forty-four. The Horseshoe Staircase, so-called for the bold baroque curves of its plan, was designed by Jean Androuet Du Cerceau and added in 1634 to the château at Fontainebleau, which had been built during the reign of Francis I (1515–47).

OPPOSITE
The magnificent grand staircase of the Paris Opera, designed by Charles Garnier (1825–98), was built 1861–74. The Opera was the largest theater building in the world, but so much space was taken up by the grand staircase and other embellishments that it does not have the largest seating capacity in Paris.

Crowds gather daily for socializing and relaxing on the famous Spanish Steps in Rome.

This etching of the Spanish Steps by Giambattista Piranesi (1720–78) reveals his training in architecture. As draftsman for the Venetian ambassador to the Papal Court, Piranesi began his long fascination with Rome, its antiquities, and its great print collection at the Vatican library. When he committed the Spanish Steps to copper plate, the ancient obelisk was not yet installed in the plaza at the head of the stairs.

OPPOSITE

The great baroque embankment of curvilinear and straight flights of stairs that compose the Spanish Steps in Rome is a dramatic meeting place and one of the world's most recognizable landmarks. In 1721 the French were granted permission by Pope Innocent XIII to build a stairway from the Piazza di Spagna to their church, Trinità dei Monti, then accessible only by steep paths up the hill. Alessandro Specchi began the project, but he was replaced in 1723 with a designer preferred by the French, Francesco de Santis, who completed the stairway two years later. The Spanish Embassy, which was located on the plaza, gave its name to both square and stairs. In this helicopter shot by adventuresome photographer Dan Budnick, the breathtaking cascade of steps ripples down the hill in the early morning sun before traffic and pedestrians engulf the Spanish Steps.

◁ Steps to the temple on the Pyramid of Kukulcan at
Chichén Itzá (Yucatan), which was founded in the
sixth century A.D. by refugees from the old Mayan
empire. The site was occupied by the Toltecs
from the twelfth to thirteenth centuries when this
pyramid was built over an older one. Four stone
stairways, one on each side of the pyramid, lead to
the temple on the summit where human sacrifices
were offered to the gods.

In the center of the Bavarian university city of
Würzburg on the Main River lies the splendid
baroque Residence Palace, which served as residence for the bishops of Bavaria and Grand Dukes
of Würzburg. Designed by the German architect
Balthasar Neumann (1687–1773) and built 1719–44,
it contains a resplendent interior staircase decorated
with magnificent frescoes by the Venetian painter
Giovanni Battista Tiepolo (1696–1770), who finished
his masterpiece in 1753.

### Top Left

The richly ornamented central ramp of this double staircase in the Forbidden City, rippling with intricately carved designs, was never meant to feel the tread of human feet. Litter bearers using the steps on either side carried the emperor over it, up the incline. Ornamented staircases lead from courtyard to courtyard throughout the huge area, which was the imperial walled fortress built within the inner city of Peking.

### Top Right

Several solid flights of stone steps lead to the summit of Dmar-po Ri, "Red Mountain" or Potala Hill, on which stand the majestic seventeenth-century buildings of the famous Potala Palace, once the fortress of the Dalai Lamas in Lhasa, the former capital of Tibet.

### Bottom

An imposing stairway of 395 granite steps leads to the mausoleum of Sun Yat-Sen, revolutionary hero, leader of the Kuomintang (nationalist party), and first president of the Republic of China. Completed in 1929, the grand mausoleum stands in the eastern outskirts of Nanjing, capital of Kiangsu Province and an important port city on the Yangtze River.

### Opposite

The Great Wall of China, which runs for a distance of 1,500 miles (2,414 km) from the Yellow Sea to Kansu, deep in Inner Mongolia, varies from twenty feet (6 m) wide at the base, twelve feet (3.5 m) at the top, and fifteen to thirty feet (4.5 to 9 m) in height, and is built of solid earth and rocks faced with brick. A twenty-five mile (40 km) portion of the Great Wall near Beijing is kept in repair for visits by both Chinese and foreign tourists. The roadway along the top of the wall has thousands of steps where the levels change sharply to conform to the contours of the earth. These stairs are difficult to climb because of the high risers and shallow treads of the steps. At 200-yard (183 m) intervals forty-foot (12 m) tall guard towers loom over the wall. Built with slave labor by Shih Huang Ti (246–209 B.C.) of the Chin dynasty, the first emperor of a united China, as defense against the Huns and other barbaric tribes to the north, the wall has been continually under repair throughout the centuries, the last extensive restoration taking place during the reign of Hsien-tung (1465–87) of the Ming dynasty.

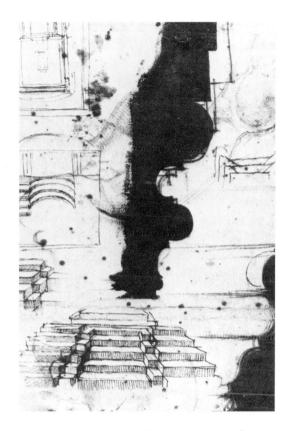

Studies by Michelangelo for the stairway and columns of the vestibule in the Laurentian Library.

This grand staircase stood in the first class lounge on the ill-fated British luxury passenger liner, *Titantic*, which struck an iceberg during her maiden voyage and sank on April 14/15, 1912, with the loss of over 1,500 lives. The wreck of the *Titantic* was discovered on September 1, 1985, by search teams from the American Woods Hole Oceanographic Institute and the Institut Français de Recherches pour l'Exploitation des Mers, collaborating in the search. Divers brought up several artifacts from the liner, among them the angel figure holding a lamp, seen at the foot of this grand staircase.

◁ Upon being elevated to Pope in 1523, Clement VII commissioned Michelangelo to design the Laurentian Library for his city of Florence, in order to return to it a collection of Medici codices. Many of Michelangelo's design studies still exist. The ornate, irrational staircase, which connected the already existing monastery of San Lorenzo to the library, rises from a small, top-lit vestibule of columns, brackets, and niches, filling the space completely.

Gleaming in white and gold with lapis lazuli columns, the main double staircase to the Hermitage is a fitting entry to the treasures that lie beyond. This great art museum adjoining the baroque Winter Palace in Leningrad was founded by Catherine the Great in 1764 and extensively refurbished (1840–52) by Czar Nicholas I.

The remarkable double spiral staircase in the stair tower of Château de Chambord in the Loire Valley, France, is built in a cage of stone at the junction of four lofty halls. The double staircase is designed to allow visitors to ascend and descend simultaneously without visual contact, though voices and footsteps can be heard. Formerly a hunting lodge, Chambord was grandly remodeled from the plans of Italian architect Domenico da Cortona, beginning in 1519, for the use of Francis I.

Tradition holds that the Scala Santa, or Holy Stairs, located near the Piazza di Porta San Giovanni in Rome, were brought to the city by Saint Helena from the palace of Pontius Pilate in Jerusalem. They were installed in the old Lateran Palace, formerly the chapel of the Popes, and have been a place of pilgrimage since the eighth century. This stairway consists of twenty-eight Tyrian marble steps (now protected by wooden boards) that some believe Jesus must have ascended for his judgment. Pilgrims climb the Scala Santa on their knees.

OPPOSITE

In 1852 the Sisters of Loretto left Kentucky trekking westward to the frontier town of Santa Fe, New Mexico, which was populated mostly by Mexicans and Indians. Mexican carpenters built them a school and some twenty years later architect P. Mouly added a gothic chapel. When construction was all but finished a serious error was discovered: through an oversight, no provision for any stairs from the beautiful chapel to its choir loft had been made. Many carpenters were consulted, but none could resolve the problem. Because the choir loft was very high above the chapel floor, conventional stairs would take up too much room. Use a ladder, they advised, or rebuild the chapel. But the Sisters had other resources: they prayed for guidance to the Master Carpenter, Saint Joseph.

As legend has it, one day a grey-haired man with a donkey appeared at the chapel and volunteered to build a staircase. Using only a saw, hammer, T-square, and a large tub of water in which pieces of wood were left to soak, he worked alone, and presently a graceful, soaring spiral staircase led to the choir loft. But when Mother Magdalene, the Sister Superior, looked for the carpenter to pay him, he was nowhere to be found. And another mystery surfaced: the local lumber yard had no record of any wood being purchased for the project.

The staircase that the old carpenter constructed for the Sisters is indeed miraculous. A spiral 22 feet high (7 m), it has no central or side supports. It has thirty-three steps, makes two complete 360-degree turns, and is fastened with wooden pegs instead of nails. Architects and builders to this day inspect the masterpiece of beauty and construction and marvel that it has not collapsed after more then one hundred years of daily use; they do not know how it is possible. The Sisters of Loretto believe they know.

In addition to their primary purpose, steps and stairs often create inviting and effective settings for varied social events, planned and spontaneous. Stairways built on the grand scale are favorite places for large ceremonial gatherings, involving hundreds of participants, since by using the stairs judiciously, dignitaries and officials can both survey the crowds and be seen by them. On a smaller scale, steps and stairs may provide a study area on campus or a brown-bag lunching spot on a mall. Stairways in public places become benches for resting and chatting and bleachers for people-watching. To enjoy the view, away from the bustle of the street, crowds seat themselves on the steps at the entrance to the Metropolitan Museum of Art in New York, in much the same way as at the Duomo in Milan, the Spanish Steps in Rome, or on the library steps of any college campus.

Steps and stairs present focal points for many social activities more important or more fanciful than simple access. Cartoonists and film makers, fascinated with the configuration of the stair, have staged comedy routines, misadventures, or dramatic incidents on them. Boys and girls, and the occasional adult, have found the temptation to slide down a banister irresistible.

People are drawn to congregate on stairs. Psychoanalyst Elliott Markoff suggests that stairs may represent "height for security, protection, and reconnaissance." At a crowded party they provide additional seating. They can also serve as a social equalizer since often the height of a single riser will bring two conversationalists eye-to-eye.

Steps and stairs are a preferred environment for recording family life. For a photographer, steps are props upon which to range the subjects, elevating them to be seen one above the other. Who has not heard or spoken the words, "Come on out, and I'll take your picture on the stairs!"? No family album would be complete without a picture of Mom, Dad, and the kids in their holiday best; or Aunt Nellie and Uncle Wilfred, leaving on their honeymoon; or one of brother Oliver clowning on the front steps. Through such varied and inventive activities, steps and stairways—originally developed as a means to provide access from one level to another—have become popular settings for our social life.

OPPOSITE
**The steps to the Metropolitan Museum of Art are often crowded with people resting or enjoying the view. Here the crowd is watching a parade on Fifth Avenue.**

◁ **In the Midlands Mall shopping center of Council Bluffs, Iowa, a multilevel sunken area—bright with lights and colored banners and a huge, unique wooden clock keeping track of time—is detached from the surrounding walking space and offers a place to relax and socialize. Astle, Ericson & Associates of Omaha were the architects.**

*199*

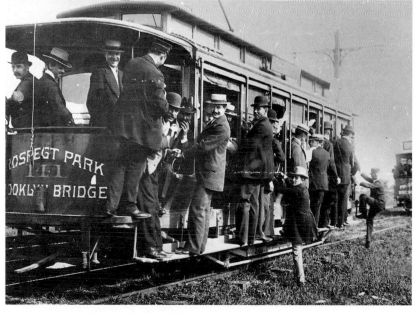

Union General Irwin McDowell and his staff posing for a group portrait on the steps of Arlington Mansion, General Lee's ancestral home. Mathew Brady took the picture shortly after the Battle of Bull Run.

OPPOSITE

Dedication of the memorial to President McKinley, assassinated by the anarchist Leon Czolgosz on September 6, 1901, was led by President Theodore Roosevelt in October 1907 and photographed by Frances Johnston. The 163-foot-tall monument, made with Milford granite and topped with a large bronze statue of the president, in the West Lawn Cemetery in Canton, Ohio, is the burial place of President McKinley, his wife, and two daughters. The imposing steps leading to the monument brought all the dignitaries attending the dedication ceremonies into the photographer's view.

◁ The step up to the Brooklyn Trolley provides a sturdy foothold for pleasure seekers bound for Coney Island in 1897.

Miss Blanche Lamont is pictured with her class on the steps to the school house at Hector, Montana, in October 1893.

BOTTOM RIGHT
The Danish king of fairy tales, Hans Christian Andersen, reading one of his stories to a crinoline-clad audience on the steps of Friisenborg Manor, 1863.

Very probably the invitation, "Come on out, and I'll take your picture on the steps," precipitated this snapshot.

A group of Japanese school boys being photographed by one of their own in front of the Great Buddha at Kamakura.

At the Tokyo Hilton, a wedding party arranged itself on the steps for a photographer, the kimono-clad ladies traditionally choosing black in order not to compete with the radiant colors of the bridal costumes.

March of Danes for March of Dimes began from the steps of the New York City Post Office in 1947, led by Danish-born Metropolitan Opera star, Lauritz Melchior (center, with fur-collared coat), and other Great Danes.

Youth choir assembled on the grand staircase of Augustusburg in Brühl during the state visit to the German Federal Republic by the President of Niger, General Seyni Kountche, in 1985.

Friends in conference, 1981.

Quentin Roosevelt, youngest son of President
Theodore Roosevelt, and friend, 1901.

Tarahumara Indians have come into town and
seated themselves on the steps of the village school
in Norogachie, Mexico, waiting for their children.

The steps to the San Antonio City Hall, Texas, were
used by the KKK in 1983 to demonstrate against
communists and illegal aliens.

On this *ghat*, Hindu for stairway, that leads to the sacred Ganges River in India, devout bathers of the Hindu faith gather for the ceremonial ritual of washing away their sins, unintentionally arranging themselves in a bright array of colors and shapes, as if positioned by the designer of a stage production.

These sturdy steps lead to the gallows at the Washington Penitentiary where Henri Wirtz, a Swiss mercenary who had been superintendent of the notorious Confederate Anderson Prison in Alabama where over 13,000 Union soldiers died, was hanged on November 10, 1865.

# Ladders

**T**he rung of a ladder was never meant to rest upon," wrote the English biologist Thomas Henry Huxley (1825–95), "but only to hold a man's foot long enough to enable him to put the other somewhat higher."

Ladders, as well as having a purely practical function, have long served as important symbols in many different cultures. They have been used as symbols of communication between heaven and earth, conveyances upon which man could ascend and the gods descend. They have been the symbol of transition between the real and the unreal; from light to darkness; from immortality to death. Thus the rungs of the ladder often represent the ascending power of human conscience.

In shamanism, the religion of the Ural-Altaic peoples of northern Asia and Europe, the shamans alone can communicate with the spirits and gods, and must ascend a ladder or a notched pole to do so. American Indians believed that the rainbow was a ladder to the world above. In the Bible Jacob's ladder symbolizes the link between heaven and earth. Falcon-faced Horus of ancient Egypt "set up a ladder to heaven among the Gods," according to the Book of the Dead, a collection of magic formulae and incantations placed in the tombs of the dead. Buddhist imagery includes a ladder often depicted with the footprint of Buddha on the bottom and top rungs suggesting the spiritual quest of the Indian philosopher, Siddhartha Gautama, who founded Buddhism. In Hebrew symbolism, a ladder is the means of communication between God and man through angels; and Islamic tradition tells of the ladder seen by Mohammed that leads true

**Commemorative photo of fire fighters' field day in Finland at the turn of the century.**

The single straight ladder has been unchanged since the beginning of recorded history. In this scene from a mural carved in 667 B.C. in the palace of King Ashurbanipal at Nineveh (near Mosul in today's Iraq), straight assault ladders are used in the seige of an Egyptian city.

TOP RIGHT
This illumination depicting the building of King Solomon's Temple from a fourth-century manuscript from Constantinople shows the ever-present straight ladder in use.

believers to Allah. Japanese belief attributes the ladder to the god of thunder and it symbolizes transit between heaven and earth. The followers of Mithra, the Persian god of light, believe that initiates ascend a ladder with seven rungs, which represents the passage of the soul through the seven heavens.

Ladders have been connected with many superstitions: climbing a ladder with an odd number of rungs is supposed to bring good luck, while walking under a ladder brings bad luck. To stand on a ladder with a pretty girl assures matrimony, while falling off a ladder not only is a misfortune but also portends a loss of money. There is one ladder everyone wants to climb, the Ladder of Success.

According to building codes, any structure for ascending or descending, standing at an angle of from 50 to 90 degrees, is defined as a ladder. Like other essential inventions, ladders come in a great variety of forms for many different uses and are made of diverse materials.

Straight or single ladders, unchanged for millennia, consist of two sidepieces (usually parallel but sometimes tapered) with rungs or treads between them. Extension ladders to reach particularly

high places are operated with or without a pull rope and stabilizing grapples. Folding double stepladders, with either a single or double set of rungs, sometimes include a painter's shelf. And there are various two-in-one-ladders, combinations of all these.

Library ladders come in all sizes, models, and designs—fixed, movable, freestanding, and on tracks. Some smaller ladders can be folded in intricate ways and even converted into pieces of furnitures.

Ladders are made for a great variety of special purposes. There are industrial ladders, fire engine ladders, and platform ladders; elephant ladders, circus ladders, and playground ladders; A-ladders, peg-post ladders, and warehouse ladders. Rope ladders, which have side pieces of rope or wire and rungs of wood, rope, or iron, include the nautical Jacob's ladders and an assortment of intricate assault ladders designed by Leonardo da Vinci. There are portable fire-escape ladders, stilt-house ladders that can be pulled up, bunk-bed ladders, and pull-down ladders, usually giving access to an attic or a roof. Human imagination has adapted the useful ladder for seemingly endless tasks.

The right sidepieces of these ladders at Taos Pueblo
in New Mexico are longer than the left to provide a
handhold when stepping off.

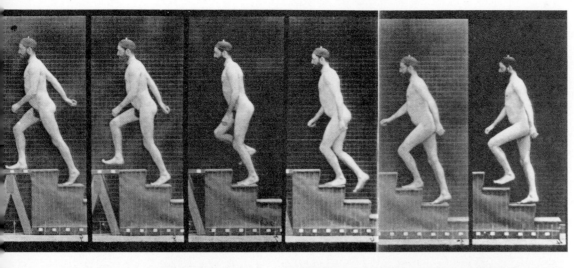

Body positions vary in direct proportion of the steepness of the stairs or ladder climbed. These studies from *Human and Animal Locomotion* (1887) by Eadweard Muybridge show the different body positions when ascending a stairway and a ladder. Other studies showing position on a normal stair appear in chapter 1.

This 1987 replica of a colonial step-chair was originally made as a dual-purpose library ladder. When safety is more important than style, stepladders may have rubber inserted or affixed to the treads to prevent slipping.

This simple wooden ladder was pictured in the book *Description et usage des principaux instruments d'astronomie* by the noted French astronomer, Pierre Charles Le Monnier (1715–99), as the means to reach the eyepiece of an early telescope.

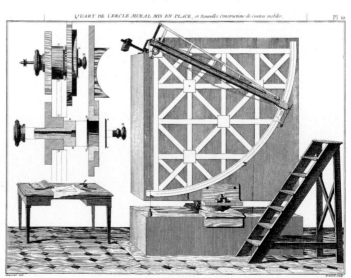

A fire engine ladder in action at a fire in Los Angeles in the 1950s.

This intricate library-table ladder was designed by Thomas Sheraton (1751–1806), English furniture designer who gave his name to a refined style of the late Georgian period. He described it as follows:

> The steps may be put up in half a minute, and the whole may be taken down and enclosed within the table frame in about the same time. The table, when enclosed, serves as a library table, and has a rising flap, supported by a horse to write on.

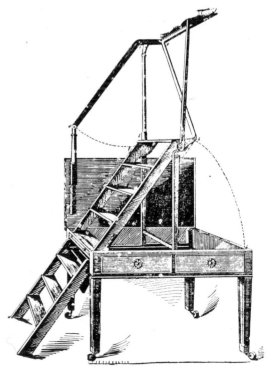

### Top Left

This simple one-room farmhouse near Pisticci, Italy, has a ladder leading to a small balcony over the entrance alcove. The farmer asked that his picture be taken while he was praying to the image of the Holy Virgin that hung over his bed.

### Top Right

This hand-hewn ladder, polished by use, rises to a loft in an old farmhouse in *Frilandsmuseet*, an open air museum north of Copenhagen, a historic reconstruction of a village showing early peasant culture in Scandinavia.

### Bottom Right

A stairway may be defined as a ladder when it becomes too steep to descend face first and necessitates a descent facing the steps, as in this residence in Norman, Oklahoma, designed by architect Herb Green.

### Opposite
### Left

With a Postmodern nod to the classic, an ingenious library stair-ladder wings up out of an arch in architect Charles Moore's own house in Los Angeles.

### Top Right

This permanent library ladder designed by Cleo Baldon for a private residence in Los Angeles leads to a cushioned seat for browsing or reading. Slots in the shelves provide additional handholds. At the far left, the lower shelves themselves are treads and risers.

### Bottom Right

Progressively deeper cuts into thick, square oak slabs form the steps of this library ladder designed by Cleo Baldon. The spiraling treads can double as shelves or afford a place to sit. The sturdy corner posts are mounted on wheels so the freestanding stair tower can be moved easily, yet be stable and safe.

Marines climb down a transport's cargo net to board landing craft during the invasion of the Marshall Islands in February 1944. Folded Jacob's ladders hang ready for use.

Climbing a Jacob's ladder, a convoy ship master returns to his ship, anchored in Hampton Roads in July 1943. The name *Jacob's ladder* has been given to three different phenomena—in nautical terminology, botany, and science. In nautical terms, a Jacob's ladder refers to a rope ladder with wooden or iron rungs used to board ships or to climb the rigging. In botany the Jacob's ladder is a perennial, ornamental herb (*Polemonium caeruleum*) native to Europe, and in science it is a device used to demonstrate electrical high voltage.

Permanent iron rungs mounted on bulkheads is another form of shipboard steps or ladders. They are strictly utilitarian and not easily negotiated, as the Wave finds out as she exits a gun mount on the USS *Missouri* during the ship's shake-down cruise in 1944.

The inimitable movie funnyman, Buster Keaton, who never did anything, even the simplest task, the way ordinary mortals would do it, here portrays the perfect lookout in the ratlines in *The Navigator* (MGM, 1924).

Sailors occasionally lay aloft for other reasons than furling or setting sails. Here the crew of a tall ship is aloft in the rigging, during the Parade of the Tall Ships in the centennial celebration of the Statue of Liberty in 1984.

This scene from *Destination Moon* (Eagle Lion, 1950) by George Pal, suggests sophisticated technology but still uses a simple ladder.

That "One small step for man, one giant leap for mankind" was off a simple ladder. During the Apollo 11 Mission, on July 21, 1969, Edwin E. (Buzz) Aldrin climbs down from the landing module, setting foot on the surface of the moon.

OPPOSITE
Satan, here portrayed by Adolphe Menjou, fallen from grace descends to his own domain via a ladder in *The Sorrows of Satan* (Paramount, 1926).

# 14 Playground Climbers

Because children love to climb, many playgrounds are equipped with a variety of steps, ladders, and climbers. Climbing equipment comes in a virtually endless variety of shapes and forms, and in climbing it, children exercise mentally as well as physically, making the equipment become whatever they want it to be—a spaceship or a fire ladder, a towering mountain or a skyscraper reached by precipitous steps.

Some steps lead to slides, tree houses, or observation platforms; others are just for climbing. Climbers are often colorful and shaped in imaginative forms: a huge snail fashioned out of a curved metal ladder, somewhat resembling a fixed hamster wheel; dragons and elephants; long-necked giraffes or covered wagons. Along with the shiny bright climbers made of painted metal or colored plastic in myriad intriguing forms, prefabricated wooden climbers are also available—from racheted, pegged, grooved, or notched timbers to block steps and climbing walls.

Play is children's work and imaginative and creative preparation for their function in the adult world. Climbers and other playground equipment are usually designed by adults, but in Emdrup, Denmark, during World War II, when no materials for building playgrounds were available, one was devised from mounds of dirt, crates and debris, bits of scrap material. Initiated and directed by landscape architect, C. L. Sørensen, it was actually built by the children themselves from their own designs, including ladders and ramps, steps and stairs to climb. When the war was over, the idea took form in Britain. In the rubble-scarred cities, play areas were set aside and scrap materials, found in the wake of war, were used to build playgrounds. Similar activity zones are today called Adventure Playgrounds. Many such playgrounds have been built with the involvement of the community and its children, including those in Golden Gate Park and the San Francisco Zoo. Commercial equipment inspired by these playgrounds is also being manufactured today. Adults who watch children at play can learn to design playgrounds as well as children do. Several playground designers have been influenced by the Adventure Playground and the equipment preferred by the children. In London, landscape architect Mary Mitchell zigzags slides down long banks of bricks or stone, in one of them setting slices of tree trunks into the slope as stairs to get to the top, in another, a cobbled bank, using outcroppings of cobbled cleats for stairs.

In New York, architect Richard Dattner designed the Adventure Playground in Central Park with a slide down the face of a bricked cone. The steps to the top are cavities where bricks have been left out. In this playground, Dattner uses amphitheaters and stair formations as divisions, as well as climbers of wood and netting. Today no playground would be complete without climbers, be it jungle gyms or piles of timbers.

**Game Time playground climber in the shape of a snail. A soft safety surface is placed under each climber to cushion any accidental fall.**

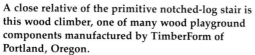

A close relative of the primitive notched-log stair is this wood climber, one of many wood playground components manufactured by TimberForm of Portland, Oregon.

TOP RIGHT
In this playground at a hospital in San Diego, architect Frank L. Hope has designed a climbing mound with footholds reminiscent of the primitive steps hollowed out of steep banks by early man.

BOTTOM RIGHT
These steps up a steep brick wall to reach a slide in a North London playground seem dangerous, although safety is usually an important concern in design and construction.

This long zigzag slide down a bricked slope,
designed by Mary Mitchell and located in London,
appeals to children's sense of adventure more than a
conventional tower slide, and it is actually safer,
because it is impossible for a child to fall vertically
from it. The top of it is reached by a series of
raised brick cleat steps set into the bricked slope.

OPPOSITE

TOP

Colorful playground climber in the shape of a bug-eyed, 22-foot (6.5 m) worm. Called a Wum by the manufacturer, Game Time, it is constructed of galvanized pipe with eyes and feeler tips of cast aluminum.

BOTTOM LEFT

A BigToys playground climber features a rope climbing net, much like cargo netting, inspired by the Adventure Playground.

BOTTOM RIGHT

On the playground of a kindergarten in a commune near Shanghai, a slide reached by a huge fish climber stands ignored, while the children go through their prescribed exercises.

This freestanding spiral slide with bucketed steps, produced by Paris Playground Equipment of Ontario, Canada, is made of steel and injection-molded polyethylene.

# 15
# Stairs in Industry

Stairs and ladders used in the space-, cost-, and efficiency-conscious world of industry are devised primarily for their functional and practical aspects, as well as for safety. Yet, their utilitarian forms often possess an inherent beauty of design.

Each industrial stair is designed for a specific task, and there are as many different configurations as there are situations in which to use them. A maze of iron stairs, usually constructed with skid-proof treads and open risers, is present on the heavy machinery used in manufacturing plants, and at warehouses or wharves. Other industrial or strictly utilitarian stairs include: peg ladders ascending telephone poles and rungs descending from manholes; steps scaling tall oil derricks and circling storage tanks; crossover platforms, much like movable stiles, used by workers to traverse large pipes or other obstacles; multilevel shipyard towers and film studio camera towers; airplane service units and the flights of rungs to service huge telescopes; as well as steps climbing industrial chimneys and town water towers; and throughout history, the military has used practical and utilitarian ladders and stairs, both portable and stationary from gun mounts to gantries.

Open-pit mine at Serra Pelada in the Brazilian Amazon forest. The sprawling excavation looks like an inside-out anthill, aswarm with workers. The system of mining recorded in this recent photo still resembles that used in Stone-Age quarries.

◁ The sun painted on this Sun Oil storage tank with its encircling stairs seems strong enough to cast real shadows.

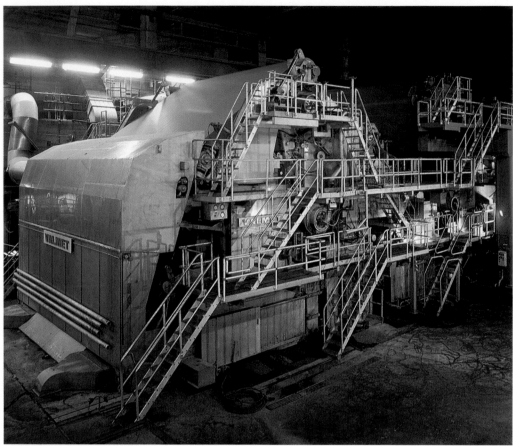

LEFT

Like a vine climbing a tree trunk, these stairs wind up the axis of a VAWT (vertical-axis wind turbine) to the height of ten floors. Unlike conventional windmills, this exotic VAWT windmill in New Mexico does not have to be pointed into the wind, but will accept it from any direction. It can generate enough electricity to service fifty homes.

TOP RIGHT

A grid of stairways makes accessible every part of this huge machine to produce printing paper, made in Finland by Valmet Machine Works.

BOTTOM RIGHT

This crossover platform works much like a portable stile.

Storage-tank ladders in the port of Oakland create an arresting pattern at sunset.

The group of soaring ladders with wire cages to
protect climbers at this 1940 refinery in El Segundo,
California, looks like the innards of a spring
mattress.

Wire cages also act as protection on these ladders to the top of a storage tank.

These unprepossessing service steps run along the prototype of a deadly device that well might have changed history had it ever been employed. The Iron Millipede, a giant gun with a barrel 492 feet (150 m) long, was installed by the Nazis at Misdroy Test Range, on Wollin Island, Germany, in 1944. It was designed to fire a large projectile with a warhead of high explosives a distance of 100 miles (160 km). Smaller lateral tubes on both sides of the main barrel, all serviced by the stairs, held explosives that boosted the main charge as the projectile traveled the length of the barrel. Because these protruding sections looked like legs on the huge cannon, it was known as the *Tausendfüssler*, or millipede. The Nazis worked feverishly to complete the tests and make the guns operative before D-Day. They missed by only a few weeks.

# 16 Stairs in Art

For artists who work in a two-dimensional medium, the use of steps and stairs, ladders, or simple risers is an effective compositional device. George Wesley Bellows (1882–1925) used an urban motif in *Cliff Dwellers*, 1913, elevating the bustling scene in the background on a series of steps, stoops, and fire escapes.

Artists and illustrators have used the ornamental and interesting planes and angles, the symmetry and sweep of steps and stairs in paintings, frequently making them a dominant feature or even the subject of a work. Often the title given a work incorporates the words *steps* and *stairs*. One such famous painting is *The Holy Family on the Steps* created in 1648 by Nicholas Poussin (1594–1665), which today hangs in the National Gallery of Art in Washington, D.C.

Sculptors as well have used the form of stairs in creating imaginative and often symbolic pieces, such as the spectacular Herbert Bayer work, *Double Ascension* (1969), which stands in a reflecting pool in Arco Square in Los Angeles.

Philatelists especially can enjoy the miniature engravings of famous buildings and their important staircases that appear on stamps from nations the world over.

*The Bridge at Trinquetaille*, 1888. A stairway to a bridge dominates this composition by Vincent van Gogh, which sold at auction in 1987 for over $20 million.

*Maria Ascending the Temple Steps* by Cima de Conegliano, an Italian painter active between 1489 and 1517. The painting was removed from a church in Venice in 1743 and now hangs in the Dresden Gallery.

*Jacob's Ladder* from *The Holy Bible with Illustrations by Gustave Doré*, published by Cassel, Peter and Galpin in London and New York, about 1866, portrays Jacob's visionary dream, which has inspired works by over one hundred renowned artists the world over, including Rembrandt, Rubens, and Carpioni.

Bible illustration by the French illustrator and engraver, Gustave Doré. Many painters have illustrated the theme of Jesus driving the money changers from the temple—among them Hieronymus Bosch, Pieter Brueghel, and Rembrandt van Rijn—and virtually all of them depicted steps or stairs in their compositions.

Study by Leonardo da Vinci of figures and architecture, including several steps and stairs, for *Adoration of the Magi*. Uffizi Gallery, Florence.

No fewer than four different staircases are visible in the brown ink and wash drawing *The Holy Family with Joseph as Carpenter*, perhaps symbolizing man's hope for ascension. The drawing by Jean de Gourmont, a French painter active 1506–51, is in the Pierpont Morgan Library Collection.

LEFT

Irish-born (1909) painter Francis Bacon has described the agonizing moments on the Odessa steps in the 1925 motion picture *Potemkin*, as one of the most important influences on his work, in which despair, violence, terror, and isolation are recurring themes. This 1971 painting of a man facing a menacing stairway is the center panel of a triptych.

RIGHT

The Victorian painter Edward Burne-Jones (1833–98) used a curved stairway without banister to bring all his beautiful subjects into unobstructed view. Designed in 1872, begun in 1876, and finished in 1880, the painting was first called "The King's Wedding" and "Music on the Stairs" until it became famous under its final title, *The Golden Stairs*. It hangs in the Tate Gallery, London.

The 28th Salon des Indépendants in Paris in 1912 refused to exhibit *Nude Descending a Stairway #2*, by Marcel Duchamp, and the painting shocked the public a year later at the Armory Show in New York. Philadelphia Museum of Art, Louise and Walter Arensberg Collection.

The stairway sculpture *Double Ascension* by
Herbert Bayer, 1969, stands in Arco Square in
downtown Los Angeles.

*Ma'alot* ("Ascent") by Ezra Orion. The sculpture,  ▷
created 1979–80, which stands in a park on a busy
highway in Jerusalem, is a simple run of stairs
erected at an exaggerated angle, thereby creating a
dissonance with the comforting familiarity evoked
by the everyday object.

In this etching, Giambattista Piranesi in 1743 created an imaginary reconstruction of the Temple of Vesta (A.D. 205) in Rome.

On the Brotherhood Building in Cincinnati, muralist Richard Haas painted a seven-story trompe l'oeil grand staircase, a classical fantasy inspired by Piranesi's etching of the Temple of Vesta.

Stairs and steps are a favored theme in the work of contemporary New York artist Brad Holland. *The Steps to the Steps* was painted in 1984.

In this urban scene, *Cliff Dwellers*, George Wesley Bellows uses foreground stairs and the stairs and landings of fire escapes in the background to carry the action to multilevel plateaus.

OPPOSITE

Among the stamps that feature stairs are Sweden's issue of *The National Museum Staircase* to commemorate the National Gallery, Blaisieholmen, Stockholm; Cuba's stamp, *Stairway and Bell Tower*, issued to commemorate the centenary of the first Cuban normal school; and the impressive stairway of the *Mayan Temple, Copan*, on a stamp issued by Honduras in 1937. Poland's stamp of the *Collegium Mauis, Cracow*, featuring its stairways, was issued in 1971 to honor the astronomer Nicolaus Copernicus; Russia issued *Subway Station, Train, and Steps* in 1934 to commemorate the completion of the Moscow subway. Other stamps featuring stairs include *Pergamum Altar of Zeus*, German Democratic Republic, 1959; *Minshia Stairs at Deir el-Kamar*, Lebanon, 1968; and *Vienna Palace of Justice*, Austria, 1984.

FIRST MAN ON THE MOON

# 17
# Stairs in Theater

Theater in its complex forms could not exist without the steps and stairs on which performers and spectators alike depend. Hellenistic and Roman theaters, usually built on a suitable natural slope or bowl, had an auditorium of rising tiers of seats, which positioned the spectators around and above the stage in a semicircle intersected by long staircases like the stays in an open fan. Their design changed little after the Theater of Dionysis, the first known permanent stone theater in the world, was built on the south slope of the Acropolis in the fifth century B.C. It could seat up to 12,000 spectators watching the works of Aeschylus and Aristophanes, Sophocles and Euripedes. The huge four-story amphitheater, the Colosseum, built in the first century on the site of the Golden House of Nero in Rome, could seat 50,000 patrons watching circus games and gladiatorial feats of combat in the arena below.

Other well preserved sites are the 7,500-seat Roman theater at Aspendus in today's Turkey; the magnificent theater of Epidaurus (ca. 350 B.C.) in Greece. In England the best-preserved Roman-built amphitheater is at Caerleon in Monmouthshire; and at Sabratha, west of Tripoli in Libya, the ruins of both a Roman theater and an amphitheater can be seen.

Modern sports stadiums conform to the basic form of the classical amphitheater: the Dodger Stadium in Los Angeles, built when the Dodger baseball team left Brooklyn for Southern California; Aztec Stadium in Mexico City, which opened in 1970 with a capacity of 104,000; Berlin Stadium, which housed Hitler's Olympics in 1936; and the new 100,000-seat Olympic Stadium built in Seoul, South Korea, for the 1988 Olympics. The same design serves outdoor theaters and concert stages, such as the 1921 Hollywood Bowl, where audiences of up to 18,000 can listen to Brahms and Beethoven, Bach and Borge under the summer stars; and the aptly named Greek Theater, also in Hollywood. They all depend on a maze of steps and stairs to provide efficient seating and good visibility. Today covered amphitheaters also exist, such as Albert Hall, built in 1867 in London, and the Madison Square Garden in New York City.

Restoration has brought back some fine old motion picture palaces, including the fabulous Fox Theater in St. Louis, Missouri, with its splendid staircase rising majestically from the lobby. The art deco balustrade of the staircase in the Wiltern Theater in Los Angeles alone is worth the visit. The Rialto Square Theater in Joliet, Illinois, called "one of the ten most beautiful theaters in the nation" when it was completed in 1925, has also been faithfully restored. Its block-long, four-story hall of mirrors is fresh once again, and the broad sweep of double stairs that circles its rotunda behind a row of columns, with its winged figure newel, is as beautiful as it was before motion pictures talked.

On the other side of the theater footlights, on stage, steps and stairs are equally important; all forms of theater employ sets that prominently include steps and stairs, desirable not only for the design possibilities they present, but because they can elevate background action so it is clearly seen. The set designed by Jo Mielziner in 1949 for Arthur Miller's *Death of a Salesman* consisted of several rooms on different levels, reached by steps and stairs, and all visible simultaneously.

*The Great Ziegfeld* (MGM, 1936) won the Best Picture Academy Award that year. The film starred William Powell, Myrna Loy, and Louise Rainer. Fanny Brice and Ray Bolger appeared in the film as themselves. The *New York Times* critic, Frank N. Nugent, said that the production number on the huge spiral piano staircase, "has never been equaled on the musical comedy stage or screen."

Perhaps the motion picture industry has made the most extensive and elaborate use of steps and stairs. Both Fred Astaire and Shirley Temple tap danced their way up and down countless elegant stairs; Scarlett O'Hara tumbled down a memorable red-carpeted staircase; Douglas Fairbanks fought off hordes of the cardinal's men on ornate palace staircases in *The Three Musketeers* (1922); Errol Flynn in *The Adventures of Robin Hood* (1938) dueled the Sheriff of Nottingham to defeat on bare and massive stone steps around a castle tower. Numerous Western heroes have battled badmen on the steps and stairs of the Old West saloons; Charlie Chaplin performed his distinctive antics on a variety of stairs and ladders; and who can forget Rocky's triumphant sprint up the seemingly endless flight of stairs to the Philadelphia Museum of Art? In the ultra-lavish film musicals of the forties and fifties, monumental and spectacular

OPPOSITE

TOP
The structure of Red Rock Amphitheater in Denver, Colorado, is very similar to that of ancient theaters.

BOTTOM LEFT
The Special Events Center (1978) at the University of Texas in Austin was designed by C/A Architects Inc., for seating flexibility. By masking off different sections a wide variety of configurations can be achieved, from a full arena stage to a proscenium stage amphitheater.

BOTTOM RIGHT
Fans muster to enjoy America's favorite pastime at Dodger Stadium.

The amphitheater in the fourth-century B.C. city of Epidaurus in southern Greece is one of the most beautiful classical theaters with both its excavated seats and steps in excellent condition. Perfect acoustics allow a speaker on the stage to be heard without raising his voice.

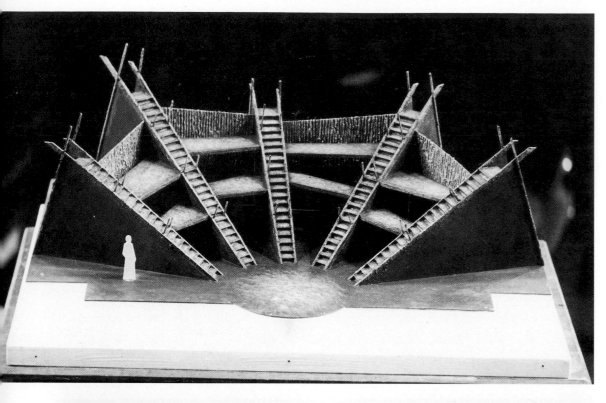

flights of stairs usually dominated the climactic scenes, often with hundreds of gorgeous show girls parading up and down the steps.

The words *steps* and *stairs* are used in many motion picture titles, including these classics: *The 39 Steps*, a Gaumont-British film starring Robert Donat and Madeleine Carroll in 1935, remade in 1960 by 20th Century Fox, with Kenneth Moore and Taina Elg; *The Spiral Staircase*, with Ethel Barrymore, George Brent, and Dorothy McGuire, RKO, 1946; *Stairway to Heaven*, starring David Niven and Kim Hunter, Universal, 1947; *The Dark at the Top of the Stairs*, a Warner Bros 1960 film of the play by William Inge, starring Robert Preston and Dorothy McGuire; *Up the Down Staircase*, Warner Bros, 1967, with Sandy Dennis; *Staircase*, 20th Century Fox, 1969, with Richard Burton and Rex Harrison.

Stairways have contributed the imagery of such song titles as "Stairway to Paradise," "Stairway to the Moon," "Stairway to the Sea," and "Stairway to the Stars." Titles of television shows also feature steps or stairs such as the mini-series, "Backstairs at the White House," "Upstairs, Downstairs," and "The Room Upstairs."

Television also makes good use of steps and stairways in its presentations, nowhere more dramatically than in the Hollywood celebration of the Academy Awards, where gorgeously dressed stars make their entrances atop a cascade of stairs. One of the most stirring moments in live television coverage occurred when Rafer Johnson, the blazing Olympic torch held high, raced up the long, long stairway at the Los Angeles Coliseum to light the flame, opening the 1984 Olympics.

OPPOSITE
TOP
This scale model of a set design shows a very elaborate and effective use of stairways to bring the action on the stage into full view. For the Opera Company of Boston's 1982 American premiere of the opera *Die Soldaten* by Bernd Alois Zimmerman, under the artistic direction of Sarah Caldwell, set designer David Sharin used five long, starkly simple staircases placed in a semicircle and leading to different levels of action.

BOTTOM
Among the sets designer Panos Aravantinos created for the premiere of the opera *The Woman Without Shadow* by Richard Strauss at the Berlin Staatsoper on April 18, 1920, this scene at the Ghost Temple shows how steps can convey a dramatic effect.

The grand staircase in the lobby of the Los Angeles Theater, a picture palace built in 1931 by S. Charles Lee that was inspired by the Hall of Mirrors at Versailles.

The sets designed by Carl Gropius for the performance of the ballet *Satanella* by Paul Tagnioni in Berlin in 1852 show a contrived use for stairs.

The Fox Theatre in Saint Louis, Missouri, has been ▷ restored, its Wurlitzer organ rebuilt, and its grand stairway polished and recarpeted in the original pattern. Built by movie mogul William Fox in 1929, the design mixes extravagant Siamese, Byzantine, Moorish, Egyptian, and other Far Eastern styles. The opulent interior features such elegant fixturing as leather-lined elevators, hand-stenciled wall coverings, intricate brass fittings, velvet-covered throne chairs, simulated marble, and gilt newel posts on the magnificent carpeted grand staircase in the lobby.

Oblivious to the menace of a platoon of the cardinal's men, Douglas Fairbanks, in unequalled exuberance slides down the banister of a palace staircase in *The Three Musketeers* (United Artists, 1921).

Basil Rathbone dueling with Errol Flynn in *The Adventures of Robin Hood*, (Warner Brothers, 1938). The spiral curves to the right so that the sword arm of the defender above could swing freely, while the attacker's right arm is hampered by the newel wall.

In the lavish operatic scene from *Two Sisters From Boston*, produced by MGM in 1946, director Henry Koster used the elaborate stairway on the set to its best advantage. The film starred June Allyson, Kathryn Grayson, Lauritz Melchior, and Jimmy Durante.

OPPOSITE

This portion of the enormous Babylonian set for D. W. Griffith's classic film, *Intolerance* (1916), represents the Palace of King Belshazzar with its several imposing staircases on which much of the action took place. One of the largest, most ornate motion picture sets ever constructed, it was so big it had to be photographed from a tethered balloon to show all of it. It stood in Hollywood, where Sunset and Hollywood Boulevards now converge, and remained for three years after the film was completed, a landmark for film buffs.

Here French singer Georges Guetary, puts his soul into the Gershwin tune "I'll Build a Stairway to Paradise" (1922) on a stairway featuring the latest word in finials. From *An American in Paris* (MGM, 1951), which starred Gene Kelly and Leslie Caron.

This famous staircase scene from Russian director Sergei Eisenstein's film *Potemkin*, 1925, was emulated in the motion picture *The Untouchables* (Paramount, 1987) when Elliott Ness desperately tried to rescue a run-away baby carriage that was lumbering step by agonizing step down an interminable staircase of Chicago's Union Station in the midst of a furious shoot-out.

This set for *Shibaraku* in the Kabuki Theater on the Ginza in Tokyo features stairs painted to look like the stone steps of a castle.

The center stage staircase is well worn because all the performers in Bali temple presentations enter via those steps.

The spiral staircase with its twisted newel in the Trumpeter's Tower of the sixteenth-century Elsinore Castle, which Shakespeare made the home of Prince Hamlet, is a good example of tread, riser, and newel cut as one. Actors Robert Breen (Hamlet) and Clarence Derwent (Polonius) appeared in a 1949 American production of the play staged at the Danish castle, and are seen here posing for a publicity shot on the staircase.

"If you find him not within this month, you shall nose him as you go up the stairs into the lobby."
*Hamlet* (Act IV, Sc. 3)

The ill-fated 1929 Erich von Stroheim silent film *Queen Kelly* displayed this classic staircase in the grand style. Filming of *Queen Kelly*, starring Gloria Swanson, stopped with only thirty percent shot when sponsor Joseph Kennedy abandoned the project because he felt that silent pictures would not be able to compete with the growing appeal of talkies. Swanson attempting to salvage the footage already filmed, contrived a make-do ending (which was promptly disavowed by Stroheim) and succeeded in having that version of the film distributed in South America and Europe, but never in the United States.

The comic possibilities of working with ladders
was not overlooked by the silent clown Charlie
Chaplin, who in the early short film *The Pawnshop*
(1916) used a ladder to great advantage.

Bela Lugosi, the ultimate vampire of motion
pictures, slinks down a sinister flight of stairs in
*Dracula* (Universal Studios, 1931).

Staircases, both interior and exterior, have always
been favorite locations for fisticuffs in films,
especially Westerns. Randolph Scott and William
Bishop in *Decision at Sundown* (Columbia, 1957).

# 18 Escalators

An escalator, whether straight or curved, is a power-driven device on which treads are mounted on a moveable stringer that forms a closed circuit. Designed like a conveyor belt, it takes passengers from one level to another with minimal effort in areas where the constant movement of crowds is necessary.

A simple moving ramp can rise at an angle of up to 15 degrees before it becomes too steep for comfort. In 1891 the American engineer Jesse Wilford Reno (1861–1947) was granted a patent on the first passenger conveyor belt with an angle of 25 degrees, possible because Reno had attached cleats to the belt, providing a foothold for the riders. Any steeper rise became too uncomfortable. Although the handrails installed on either side were stationary, moving handrails were soon developed. This type of passenger conveyor belt became known as the Reno-type escalator. About the same time, Charles D. Seeberger brought out a conveyor that had horizontal moving treads, and the grade of rise could be increased. The Otis Elevator company acquired both these patents and installed its first models in 1900 at the Paris Exhibition as well as in the New York subway and at Bloomingdale's department store in New York City. The word *escalator*, originally a trademark of Otis, was adjudged in 1949 to have entered the public domain through everyday use.

In comparison with the elevator, the escalator has several advantages as a people mover: it has a larger handling capacity for short distances; it is immediately available—passengers do not have to wait for it to arrive; it requires less installation space than the banks of elevators that would be required for comparable transport; and it is less costly to run.

Most escalators move at a rate between 90 and 120 feet (27 to 37 m) per minute. The capacity of the escalator depends on the width of the tread. The standard sizes are 32 and 48 in. (81 and 122 cm) measured between the side balustrades. Treads of the maximum width enable the escalator to move up to 12,000 people per hour.

The escalator incline is typically 30 degrees and it is generally limited to the average floor to ceiling height, about 12 feet (3.5 m), although there are spectacular exceptions. At the Woodley Park Zoo Station of the Washington, D.C., Metro the escalator flight is 204 feet (62 m) long and rises to the height of a ten-story building, proportions made possible by advanced technology.

OPPOSITE
**Multihued lighting in the ceiling of this escalator in the Detroit Science Center creates a futuristic effect of great visual impact, turning the short trip into an adventure in color and illumination. A variety of different color schemes can be produced by the lighting in the Luxalon Ceiling System by Hunter Douglas, Inc.**

**Riding the great escalator enclosed in a huge transparent tube that zigzags up the side of Le Centre d'Art et Culture Georges Pompidou, designed by Richard Rogers and Renzo Piano, is a magical ride as the city of Paris is gradually revealed beneath.**

Moving escalator steps, consisting of a continuous series of treads and frames attached to chains, are built between two side enclosures, which serve as railings and conceal the mechanism. Each separate step is constructed as an individual carriage with four small wheels set in pairs, which run on separate tracks, the top pair set a little farther out than the bottom pair. In the middle of the circuit, the two tracks are situated in the same plane; near the top and bottom reversal points, the tracks change position, so the inner track falls below the outer one. This results in the treads gradually merging into a flat surface at the top and rising to form individual steps at the bottom, as the belt makes its turn. Thus passengers can step on and off the moving steps easily and safely.

The escalator is now widely used, because it is so efficient. In addition to its effectiveness as a functional device, the design of escalators makes possible aesthetic solutions quite different from those used for conventional staircases.

"Just stand still, Joey. The stairs walk you."

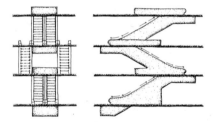

**Parallel configuration**

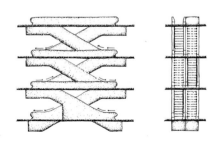

**Crisscross configuration**

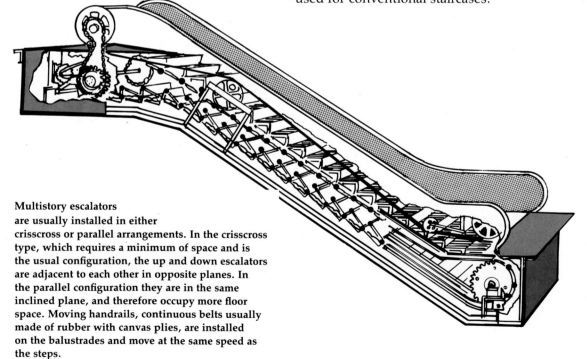

**Multistory escalators** are usually installed in either crisscross or parallel arrangements. In the crisscross type, which requires a minimum of space and is the usual configuration, the up and down escalators are adjacent to each other in opposite planes. In the parallel configuration they are in the same inclined plane, and therefore occupy more floor space. Moving handrails, continuous belts usually made of rubber with canvas plies, are installed on the balustrades and move at the same speed as the steps.

Escalators in a shopping center in Vienna add an
interesting design element and offer convenience to
shoppers.

The escalator in the Boca Beach Club Hotel &
Cabanas in Boca Raton, Florida, is covered with
softly tinted laminated glass.

Escalator in the Pacific Design Center in Los
Angeles designed by Cesar Pelli. The building,
affectionately dubbed the Blue Whale, is covered
entirely in blue glass panels. These escalators,
constructed in neither the popular parallel nor
crisscross configurations, require the passengers to
walk around the entire escalator structure at each
floor.

A richly appointed escalator rises in the soaring
daylit lobby space of New York's opulent Trump
Tower.

Escalator in the Lotte department store in Seoul

A curved escalator in Shopping Center CREO in Tsukuba, Japan, shows the latest advance in escalator design. Mitsubishi Electric developed the first such escalator, which was installed in the futuristic Science City at Tsukuba in 1985. The concept and quest for a practical escalator that could move passengers on a curved plane is not new. Already in 1906 an experimental device—the Reno Helical Moving Stairway—was installed in the Holloway Road Station in London. It was apparently not successful as only one photograph has survived and all data have been lost. The challenge of how to solve the safety and durability problems of a true helical escalator as well as the coordination of the movements of steps and handrails remained. In 1974, Gilbert Luna, a thirty-year-old California inventor, brought about a second important breakthrough when he presented a working model of a curved escalator. Questions of safety, longevity, and coordinated movements lingered, however, and Luna's concept, while contributing much innovative engineering, was considered too complicated for production at the time. The evolution of computer science during the following decade made it possible to solve the problems inherent in both the Reno and Luna concepts, and the spectacular helical escalator is now reality. But, maintains Mitsubishi engineer Shigeru Goto: "Without today's computers the project could not have succeeded."

# Index

# Photo Credits and Permissions

City where a photographer is located may be given only at first reference.

**Jacket** Scala/Art Resource, N.Y.C.

1-Frank Wing/The Image Bank, L.A. 2-Dana Levy, L.A. 4-Jaime Ardiles-Arce, N.Y.C. 6-Henk Snoek, London 10-Julius Shulman, L.A. 11-Library of Congress

**Chapter 1** 14-Yukio Futagawa, Tokyo 15L-Ole Malling, Lejre, Denmark 15R-Schloss Gottorf, Schleswig-Holsteinisches Landesmuseum 17-Philadelphia Museum of Art, Louise & Walter Arensberg Collection 18-*The Basic Writings of Sigmund Freud*, Modern Library of Random House, Inc., translated and edited by Dr. A. A. Brill, 1938, renewed 1965 Gioia B. Bernheim, Edmund Brill. Reprinted by permission 18–19L, R-Julius Shulman

**Chapter 2** 22-Ben Wittick, Museum of New Mexico (16043) 24T-University Museum, U. of Pennsylvania 24B-Art History Museum, Vienna 25-Tohuru Nogami/Kodansha, Tokyo 26-Christine Adler, L.A. 27L-Zev Radovan, Jerusalem 27R-Mus. of N.M. (8213) 28-Richard Rowan Collections Inc. Miami, FL 29-Christine Adler, 30L-Sy Edelstein, Venice, CA 30R-Art Resource, N.Y.C. 30B-Pergamon Museum, East Berlin 31-Roloff Beny, National Archives Canada 32T-Barry Howe, Laguna Hills, CA 32B-Julius Shulman 33-Joanne Van Tilburg, Malibu, CA

**Chapter 3** 34-Michael Black, London 36B-Cleo Baldon, 36RT,L–37T,B-Dana Levy, L.A. 37R-Robin Constable Hanson, L.A. 38T,M-Cleo Baldon 38B-Julius Shulman 38R-Henry D. Tefft, Mus. of N.M. (105932) 39-Julius Shulman 40L-David Glomb, L.A. 40R-The Preservation Society of Newport County 41-Marbleworks, L.A. 42L-Paul Cavallaro, L.A. 42RT-Hileman, Jones Collection, Glacier National Park 43-Julius Shulman 44L-Michael Alexander, S.F., CA 44R-Noel Norskog, Santa Fe, NM 45-Julius Shulman 46L-Henrich Blessing, Chicago 46T-Signatures in Acrivue, L.A. 46B-Julius Shulman

**Chapter 4** 48-Dennis Stock/Magnum, N.Y.C. 49-Cleo Baldon 50T-Julius Shulman 50B-Cleo Baldon 51-William Carter, Palo Alto, CA 52T-Cleo Baldon 52B-Julius Shulman 52R-Ezra Stoller/Esto, Mamaroneck, NY 53-Andreas Feininger, N.Y.C. 54L-Meiji Jingu 54R-Ib Melchior, L.A. 55L-Dana Levy, L.A. 55R-Yukio Futagawa 56T-Cleo Baldon 56B-Dana Levy, L.A. 57-Julius Shulman 59-John Halardes, Chicago 60-Julius Shulman 61-L,TR,BR Tom Luckey, Bradford, CT

**Chapter 5** 62-Cary Hazlegrove, Nantucket 63-Dana Levy, L.A. 64T-Robert Pressman, L.A. 64B-Cleo Baldon 65T-Chantal Howard, Paris 65B-Mick Hales, Hoboken, NJ 66-Mus. of N.M. (80836) 67-Ruben V. Burrell/Hampton U. Archives, VA 68L-Cleo Baldon 68T-Dana Levy, L.A. 68B-Julius Shulman 69-Dana Levy, L.A. 70L-Whitney Cox, N.Y.C. 70R-Essex Institute, Salem, MA 71-Julius Shulman 72R-Jaime Ardiles-Arce 72T-Ib Melchior 72B-Christine Adler 73-Franz Hubmann, Vienna 74L-David Glomb/Home Magazine Publishing Corp. 74R-Peter Paige, N.Y.C. 75-Julius Shulman

**Chapter 6** 76-Julius Shulman 78-Dana Levy, L.A. 79-Michele Burgess, Huntington Beach, CA 80-Julius Shulman 81T,B-Dana Levy, L.A. 81R-Carol Simowitz, S.F., CA 82-Chantal Howard, Paris 83L-D.T. De Domenico, Berkeley 83M-Dana Levy, L.A. 83R-Cleo Baldon 84-Norman Carver, Kalamazoo, MI 85LT-Andreas Feininger 85B,R-Norman Carver 86L-Julius Shulman 86R-Michael Yamashita, Mendham, NJ 87-Cliff Hollenbeck, Seattle, WA 88-J. Feuillie, Paris/C.N.M.H.S./S.P.A.D.E.M. 89-Sydney Opera House Trust 90L,RT-Julius Shulman 90RB-Cleo Baldon 91L,R-

Adam Woolfit/Woodfin Camp, N.Y.C. 92L-Ib Melchior 92M-Julius Shulman 92R-Ib Melchior 92B-N.Y. Historical Society (23611) 93T-Rick Tunell, Studio City, CA 93B-Internationes Photo Archive, Bonn 94TL,B-Christine Adler 94TR-Ria Drahnam, Los Gatos, CA 95L-Michele Burgess 95R-Michael Yamashita 96L-Julius Shulman 97-Dana Levy, L.A. 98T-Julius Shulman 98BL-Dave Phillips, Dover Books, NY 98BR M. C. Escher c/o Cordon Art, Baarn, Holland 99-L,R Library of Congress 100L-Jim Mitchell, San Antonio, TX 101-Christine Adler 102-Julius Shulman 103L-Norman Carver 103R–104L-Julius Shulman 104R-Glen Allison, L.A. 105-Richard Bryant/Arcaid, Surrey, Eng. 106L-Henrich Blessing 106R–107BR-Julius Shulman 108-Peter Aaron/Esto 109-Harvey Croze 1946/Cranbrook Archives

**Chapter 7** 110-Dana Levy, L.A. 111-Julius Shulman 112-Ib Melchior 113-Art Resource 114L-Dana Levy, L.A. 114R-Glen Allison 115TL-Dana Levy, L.A. 115R-Robin Constable Hanson 115B-Cleo Baldon 116L-N.Y. Historical Soc. 116R-Luc Meichler, Paris 116B-Julius Shulman 117-Dumbarton Oaks 118TL-Dana Levy, L.A. 118TR-Ken Druse, Brooklyn, NY 118BL-Lucian Niemeyer, Aston, PA 118BR-Carol Simowitz 119-Mick Hales

**Chapter 8** 120-Robert Winslow, Durango, CO 121-Hebrew U. Jerusalem 122L-Zev Radovan, Jerusalem 122R-Oriental Institute, U. of Chicago 123T-Peter Grant, L.A. 123BL-Michael Yamashita 124L-Letitia Burns O'Connor, L.A. 124R-Bath City Council 125L,TR,BR-Dana Levy, L.A. 126T-Robert Holden, London 126BL-Sebastian Giefer, L.A. 126BR–127B-Dana Levy, L.A. 127T-Paul Cavallaro 128T,R-Julius Shulman 129-John Blades/Hearst, San Simeon, State Historical Monument

**Chapter 9** 130-Trustees of the Chatsworth Settlement, Bakewell, Derbyshire 132–133-Art Resource 134T–135-Internationes Photo Archives 136BL-Paul Cavallaro 136R-Public Information Office, State Capitol, Des Moines, IA 137-Museum of the City of New York 138L-Jeremy Marks/Woodmansterne, Watford, Herts, Eng. 138R-Library of Congress 139-Jindrich Folfin, Vienna 140L-Trustees, Sir John Soane's Museum 140R-British Tourist Authority, N.Y.C. 141-Julius Shulman 142-Shaker Village 143TL-Winchester Mystery House 143BL-Jan Jensen, Topsfield, MA 143R-David Franzen, Honolulu 144L-Royal Library, Copenhagen 144M-Linda L. Legaspi, Miami, Fl 144R-John M. Roberts, Portland, OR 145-Yukio Futagawa 146L-Julius Shulman 146R-Mike Quan/Light Image, Mill Valley, CA 147L-Glen Allison 147R-Richard Bryant/Arcaid 148L-Chanel, Paris 148R-Strüwing Reklame Foto Birkerød, Denmark 149-Yukio Futagawa/Retoria 150L,R-The Preservation Society of Newport County 151–152L,R–153-Julius Shulman 154R-DMB&B, Milan 155-Glen Allison 156T,B–157-Julius Shulman 158-Dick Busher, Seattle, WA 159-The Mission Inn 160L-David Zanzinger, Santa Monica, CA 160R–161-Julius Shulman

**Chapter 10** 162–163-Julius Shulman 164L-Dana Levy, L.A. 165M-Tyler Dingee, Mus. of N.M. (22866) 166-Public Information Office, State Capitol, Des Moines, IA 167-Scala/Art Resource, N.Y.C. 168T-Royal Library, Copenhagen 168B-Brian Feeney, Statue of Liberty Nat'l. Monument 169-Royal Botanic Gardens, Kew 170L-Julius Shulman 170M-Jerome Rosenburg, L.A. 170R-Andy Gammon, Lewes, Sussex, Eng. 172L-Howard Detwiler 172M-Cleo Baldon 172R-Julius Shulman 173-Gabrielle Basilico, Milan 175L-Andy Gammon 175M-Bo Parker, N.Y.C. 175R-Cleo Baldon 176L,R-Julius Shulman 178B-Jean-Marie Monthiers, Paris 179-Ken Kirkwood, Stoke, Albany, Leicestershire, Eng. 180-Mark Darley, N.Y.C.

**Chapter 11** 182-Yukio Futagawa/Retoria 184–185-J.Feuillie/C.N.M.H.S./S.P.A.D.E.M. 186TL-Leo de Wys, Inc./Steve Vidler 187-Dan Budnick, East Hampton, NY 188-Julius Shulman 189-Lauros/Giraudon/Art Resource 190–191T-Barry Howe 191BL-Dana Levy, L.A. 191BR-Bernice Curler, Fair Oaks, CA 192-Art Resource 193R-Charles Sachs, Studio City, CA 194-Rick Tunell 195L-Art Resource 195R-Robin Constable Hanson 196-Dana Levy, L.A. 197-Lord Studio, Mus. of N.M. (14722)

**Chapter 12** 198-Stan Ries/Leo de Wys, N.Y.C. 199-Joel Strasser, Sioux Falls, SD 200–201T-Library of Congress 201B-Museum of the City of N.Y. 202T-Library of Congress 202R-Henrik Tileman/Odense City Museum 203T-Dana Levy, L.A. 203B-Mike Yamashita 204B-Internationes Photo Archives 205L-Library of Congress 205R-Cleo Baldon 206R-Jim Markham, San Antonio, TX 206L-Ava Vargas, Hampton, Eng. 207T-Dick Sharpe, L.A. 207B-Alexander Gardner/Library of Congress

**Chapter 13** 208-Collection Åbo Akademi, Åbo, Finland 210-The British Museum, London 211-Julius Shulman 212L-The Old Wagon Factory, Clarksville, VA 212R-Special Collections, State U. Library, San Diego, CA 213-Frank Manwarren Collection, Glendale, CA 214TL-Norman Carver 214TR-Ib Melchior 214B-Julius Shulman 215L-Sebastian Giefer 215TR-Dick Sharpe, L.A. 215BR-Julius Shulman 216L,M,R-Dept. of the Navy, Wash., D.C. 217L-Guy Gurney, New Canaan, CT 218B-NASA

**Chapter 14** 220-Tucker Wayne/Luckie, Birmingham, AL 222TR-Julius Shulman 222B–223-The Design Council, London 224T-Tucker Wayne/Luckie 224BR-Ib Melchior

**Chapter 15** 226-Anspach Grossman Portugal Inc., N.Y.C. 227-Richard Kozak, Insite Mag. 228L-Sandia Lab, Albuquerque, NM 228TR-Consulate General of Finland, L.A. 228BR-Lapeyre, New Orleans, LA 229-Robert Steve Bauer, Oakland, CA 230-Julius Shulman 231L-Cleo Baldon 231R-Archives, Fed. Republic of Germany

**Chapter 16** 232-Christie's, N.Y.C. 234L-Art Resource 236L-Francis Bacon, Marlborough, London 238L-Paul Cavallaro 238R-Uri Mueller, Tel Aviv 239L-Peter Mauss/Esto 239TR-courtesy Academy Editions, London 240B-Los Angeles County Museum of Art 241-Dana Levy, L.A.

**Chapter 17** 244T-Carl Purcell, Alexandria, VA 244BL-Richard Payne, Houston, TX 244R-Richard Kee, L.A. 245-Dana Levy, L.A. 246T-Fay Foto Service, Boston, MA 247-Henry E. Huntington Library, San Marino, CA 249-Maritz Communication Co./Fox Assoc. 253T-Michael Yamashita 253B-Christine Adler 254L-Poul Froling/A.P.

**Chapter 18** 256-The Siesel Co., N.Y.C. 257-Glen Allison 258T-Hank Ketcham, Monterey, CA 258BL-Lisa Chestnut, L.A. 259L,R–260L-Julius Shulman 260R-Carol Simowitz 261T-Michael Yamashita